INSIDE SCHOOL TURNAROUNDS

Inside School Turnarounds

Urgent Hopes, Unfolding Stories

Laura Pappano

Harvard Education Press
Cambridge, Massachusetts

HARVARD EDUCATION LETTER
IMPACT SERIES

Library of Congress Control Number 2010931407

Paperback ISBN 978-1-934742-74-7
Library Edition ISBN 978-1-934742-75-4

Published by Harvard Education Press,
an imprint of the Harvard Education Publishing Group

Harvard Education Press
8 Story Street
Cambridge, MA 02138

Cover Design: Perry Lubin
The typefaces used in this book are Adobe Garamond Pro and Scala Sans.

For my grandfather, the late Dr. George Svehla, who during four decades as a Cleveland Public School teacher taught economics, history, English, bookkeeping, shorthand, typing, and business practices and also managed the school bookstore, coached the rifle team, and conducted research that reflected his worries about the plight of poor urban teens. Some of his concerns, including those about students quitting high school to take low-paying jobs, resonate today.

CONTENTS

ACKNOWLEDGMENTS

Like school turnaround, this book was written quickly—with a lot of help and a great deal of blind faith that what I was trying to do would work. Fortunately, there is no set of test scores to announce success or failure, although judgment will come in some form, I'm sure. I make this point because while I relied on the generosity of more than sixty people willing to speak, supply data, reflect with utter frankness on change in the midst of leading it, I alone am responsible for whatever shortcomings or flaws this book contains. The process of writing a book essentially on deadline is tricky and, by its nature, doesn't allow time for the level of review and reflection that makes me comfortable. However, I understand the need and value of reporting and writing quickly, capturing turnaround in the moment in which it is unfolding. I can only hope that I have done a fair job of balancing breaking news with accuracy and insight.

I owe incredible thanks to those who allowed me into their schools and classrooms and took time from pressured and packed days to arrange meetings and speak with me about what they were trying to accomplish. Thanks to David Medina in Hartford for scheduling, answering lists of questions, and gathering data. Thanks to Joe Nathan at the Center for School Change at Macalester for the many conversations, e-mails, and nudges to get others on board. This book is largely based on in-person reporting and interviews (both telephone and in-person) I conducted between November 2009 and April 2010. Quotes throughout the book attributed to speakers are the result of interviews or notes I took while reporting. I have changed the names of children under eighteen to protect their privacy. All adults are identified by their real names, as are students from the Hartford Public High School focus group quoted or mentioned in the book. Thank you to those who agreed to be interviewed, allowed me to report, or offered helpful conversations, including: Steve Adamowski, Christina Kishimoto, Joan Massey, Adam Johnson, John Hayes, Jacqueline Ryan, Tory Niles, Charlene Senteio, Terrell Hill, David Gay, Stacey McCann, Karen Gray, Bridget Allison, Mark Oakman, Linda Tran, Kathryn McEachern, Yvonne D'Eliseo, Carol Wright, Heidi Bothamly, Kerry Swistro, Andrea Johnson, and the many students in Hartford and Revere schools who took time to share their thoughts and observations, including our Hartford Public High School focus group, comprised of Danny Contreras, Carlanna Dyer, Shaquana Cochran, and several classmates. Thanks to Gabriel Rosario, Yesenia Rosario, Eric Schwarz, Patrick Kirby, Megan Bird, Emily Stainer, Stacey Gilbert, Dawn MacDonald, Todd Litton, Meredith Lowe, Erin Dreisbach, Paul Dakin, Amrita Sahni, Monica Caporale, Julie Venditti, Diana De La Rosa, Mandy Haeuser, Jack Cassidy, Sharon Johnson, Anthony Smith, Michael Turner, Gloria Ononye, Carolyn Martinez, Kathleen Ware, Jocelynne Jason, Sandy Houck, Cheryle Kelleher, Elizabeth Holtzapple, Janet Walsh, Jeanna Jones, Lisa McLaughlin, Steve Mancini, Furman Brown, Scott Given, Dacia Toll, Ellen Guiney, Andrew Calkins, Justin Cohen, and Alex Johnston for a lot of good discussion.

I am grateful to Robert Schwartz, academic dean of the Harvard Graduate School of Education, who offered early guidance and support, and to Thomas Payzant, professor at the Harvard Graduate School of Education and former superintendent of the Boston Public Schools. My dear friend and former school foundation president, Mandy Bass, took time—on deadline, no less—to read and comment on the first draft and raised key questions (and caught errors before I embarrassed myself). Nancy Walser offered the initial nudge to do this project and, later, insight and important commiseration conversation when the deadline was arriving way too fast. My editor, Caroline Chauncey, has a way of being sympathetic and encouraging at the same time that she doesn't shrink from posing tough questions and picking up those bits of writing that overreach and need to be reined in. Thank you.

And, of course, special thanks to my husband, Tom, and my children, Olivia, Molly, and Donovan, not just for being so independent and understanding (including leaving me alone with my laptop during all of spring break and more) but for asking really good questions and helping me debrief and think through what I was seeing and hearing each day I came back from reporting. You are the best.

FOREWORD

Deep in our collective sense of the promise of America is the notion that every American—no matter who they are or what their family's social standing—has an opportunity to succeed. As a nation we make that opportunity real and tangible through the institution of public schools; public schools that don't deliver on that promise imperil not only the futures of their students but the very foundations of our democracy.

All that may seem a bit overly theoretical to a teacher faced with students who are ill-housed, ill-clad, and ill-nourished and who may simply seem to need a kind word and a good meal. But public school teachers bear an almost sacred duty to help even the poorest of children gain access to the vast opportunities that exist in this country. Teachers are, in a sense, guides to future generations of citizens; for our poorest and most isolated children, public school teachers are sometimes the only guides available.

That is why, when educators say—and far too many of them do— that by the time many poor children arrive at the schoolhouse door it is already too late to help them catch up, they are part of a profound betrayal of the idea of America. Not that those educators are solely to blame; for too long they have been told by academics, policy makers, and others that there was very little they could do to combat the forces of poverty and isolation. And they have had to operate within an institutional structure that, in the harshly bracing words of Harvard University's Richard Elmore, "is deliberately and calculatedly incompetent at influencing its core functions."

In recent years, however, it has become crystal clear that schools do have it within their power to help not just a few outstanding kids who happen through the doors of high-poverty schools but all kids—even unprepossessing children from hapless families.

Careful study has demonstrated that three really good teachers in a row can lift kids way past ordinary learning trajectories; three bad teachers in a row can devastate the life chances of children whose families are unable to intervene effectively.

But it is not enough simply to talk about good and bad teachers. Teachers develop within their preparation programs, the schools in which they teach, and their districts, all of which have enormous power and influence over whether teachers are effective or ineffective and thus whether children learn a lot or a little.

Some schools and districts, for example, understand how crucial they are in the lives of their students and make sure teachers have the help and support they need to teach effectively. Others have an appropriate understanding of the urgency of their work but not the necessary skill and knowledge to help their teachers, resulting in teachers who feel overwhelmed and undermined. And still others operate as if they were in a time warp, claiming that all is fine and allowing teachers to feel that there's nothing they need to do to change, even though most teachers are pretty sure *something* needs to change.

All of which makes now an exciting time to be an educator in this country, though it must sometimes feel like the "interesting times" of the purported ancient Chinese curse.

That precarious excitement is what Laura Pappano captures in this book: urgency clashing with complacency, new expectations colliding with long-established practice.

Pappano has chosen her subjects well. For example, Hartford, Connecticut, has long been one of the school districts that cause despair. One of the poorest cities in the country in one of the richest states, Hartford has had dismal academic achievement for decades. But in the last few years, under the leadership of Superintendent Steven Adamowski, there have developed reasons to hope. Just to give a couple of examples: in 2006 only 44 percent of the district's seventh graders met state math standards; in 2009, 60 percent. In 2006 only 46 percent of the city's eighth graders met state reading standards; in 2009, 52 percent. This is not startling improvement, and Hartford is certainly not anywhere near where it should be as a district. But it is now inching its way forward instead of steadily falling behind. That is noteworthy in part because so few districts have managed to make whole-district progress. With more than 22,000 students in forty-six schools, Hartford is not the biggest battleship in the public education world, but it is still hard to turn. And Hartford appears to be turning.

Pappano provides a nice overview of the policy context in which administrators like Adamowski are operating and gives us glimpses into what it looks like to watch a superintendent turn a system upside down and inside out. Some of what she documents made me cheer; some made me wince. She has captured the hope that public schools can be shaped to serve all the children in them; she has also managed to capture the understanding that the education field hasn't yet figured out how to do that and desperately needs infusions of knowledge and skill in order to fulfill its mission. She gives a sense of the chaos of a district that is trying something—anything—rather than allowing itself to continue its torpor. And she keeps well in sight the sense that the policy world, so desperate for answers, sometimes seizes on anything that seems promising and begins force feeding it down the chain of command, even when it is completely inappropriate for some schools.

To ensure that we don't waste this moment when the nation as a whole seems to understand the importance of public education, it is crucial to study what is happening in the world of school reform and subject it to a critical eye. This book is a timely contribution to the understanding of what works and what doesn't so that, as Pappano says, we can "inject sanity and sustainability into radical school reform."

—Karin Chenoweth
Senior writer, The Education Trust
August, 2010

1

THE TURNAROUND HOPE

ADAM JOHNSON, PRINCIPAL OF THE Law and Government Academy at Hartford Public High School, has found a new tool: a small, red spiral-bound notebook that slips easily into his dress shirt pocket. It may be its newness, or the explosion of problems that present themselves in an urban high school, but every few minutes he pulls it out and makes notes in blue marker. "I find myself writing down everything," he comments.

In 2008, after years of poor performance in which less than two-thirds of students who started ninth grade at Hartford Public High actually graduated, the district closed the school of 1,579 students (over 95 percent of whom were eligible for free or reduced-price lunches and 98.1 percent minority). In the same space, the district opened four new, smaller schools, including the Law and Government Academy. Johnson's job—as it is for principals trying to untangle the failures in urban schools across America—is complicated but critical.

Taking a moment to retreat to his office, Johnson flips through the pages of his notebook. As he shares its contents, he unwittingly offers a snapshot of what school turnaround looks like at ground level. "Here's a kid who says her teacher is refusing to give her a progress report. Here is a kid who has his pants sagging down his butt. Here is a kid who wants to go to adult ed—he's been expelled twice." The list ranges from the relatively trivial, but symbolic, items to issues that collide with policy debates within reform. Daniela Jones is wearing sneakers (instead of the dress-code-required black shoes); Maria Ramirez wants graffiti removed from her locker. But Johnson also wonders in a notation, "Compact kids?" This refers to how they should handle students who are, he says, "not cutting it." These students could drag down test scores and, critically, the school's expected gains in performance, threatening its survival.

This is one of those below-the-radar struggles in school turnaround. While failing kids need a lifeline, Johnson doesn't want those students who are seriously seizing on reform to build real futures for themselves to be derailed by kids who put in little effort and cause trouble. In other words, does turnaround mean you change the outcome for *everyone* or just for those willing to work at it? "We are trying to say, 'Are we going to disinvite kids?'" explains Johnson.

He has also jotted down a worry about the toll of turnaround work on his dean of students, who has become so involved that "he is absorbing a lot of kids' emotional baggage and taking it on himself." Then there is the need to attend to the expectation that Johnson get students ready for college in a district in which only 41 percent read at grade level. Not just "ready" in the abstract sense but tangibly. For example, there is a financial aid workshop scheduled today for all seniors, and with a single counselor, he says, "I am scrambling to figure out how to get all 105 kids through this process."

Johnson, a Harvard Graduate School of Education alum, comes across as a thoughtful crusader charging down the hallways and attending to details (the notes) while fully aware that he is not just leading a school but running a live experiment: can the worst schools in America be made dramatically better? Johnson is not fully sure of the answer. "There is a very, very interesting story to be told, but it's not done yet," he says as he sets up a booth for a citywide school choice fair. "We could still fail. We are doing some good things with our kids, but I see some ways in which we could be blown to shreds."

Turnaround up Close

As Johnson understands, more than a year into his turnaround effort there is a lot of uncertainty about how it will turn out. Originally, the goal of this book was to pull together what was *working* in school turnaround. But it quickly became obvious that this information did not exist in definitive form, and would not for years. While there is help and guidance out there, and there are good examples of schools that have raised and sustained student achievement, typically this has happened over years and in a different climate than we have today.

School turnaround—this adrenaline-charged moment that we are presently in—is about rapid and dramatic improvement not just in test scores but also in culture, attitude, and student aspirations. It is marked not by orderly implementation but by altering a lot at once and being willing to step in and change—and change again. It is a new paradigm for education, one not about trusting the process but about seeking results, both measurable and immeasurable. This does, as Johnson suggests, make for a good story.

This book attempts to capture school turnaround as it is happening. When you visit schools, talk to education leaders, principals, parents, students, or simply walk through hallways, step into teachers' lounges, or sit in the back of classrooms, you come across truths. You see different things than what are described in reports and how-to guides about school turnaround. For those in the midst of school turnaround, a lot of decision making happens in the moment and some actions come out of commonsense ideas based in personal experience. Inevitably, there are struggles and tensions.

My goal for this book is to offer a window into the work of those deeply involved in school change. I hope that in sharing their experiences, these stories-in-progress—some mere snapshots or ideas being tried and tested—will provide guidance and inspiration as well as a means for viewing the complexity of this undertaking. This is a special moment in the history of education, one in which productive work may well provide a new trajectory for the disappointing path of urban schooling. It is a time of opportunity, but certainly not of guarantees. It matters that we get this right. I hope this book will offer affirmation of some approaches, rejection of others, benchmarks for judging progress, and, perhaps most simply, some ideas worth thinking about and some people worth meeting.

I have tried to orient stories and observations to the larger purpose of turnaround and link ideas to the goal of dramatically raising the academic achievement and life opportunities for children in high-poverty schools. This book draws on different voices—from education experts and charter school leaders to district leaders, principals, teachers, parents, and students, among others—and on data from demographics to test score results. Even as theories abound about turnaround strategies, I have tried to remain concrete. The questions in my mind are: How will this help? What is *really* happening here? Is what they are doing working? If not, why? How do they do it?

The reporting for this book offers a narrative thread while, at the same time, hits on key questions in turnaround. For that reason, much of my reporting, including interviews and observations, took place at various schools in Hartford, Connecticut, because the district, held up as an example of model turnaround efforts by U.S. Secretary of Education Arne Duncan, provided me the opportunity to see different reform strategies in action. In Hartford, some schools know they are closing down yet still have teachers working and children attending. Some are merging. Others, like the Law and Government Academy, are opening as new schools but in an old space and with many of the same students. Hartford also has charter providers, including Achievement First, that are independent but work within some district parameters. The district reflects the boldness of its school superintendent, Steven Adamowski, who comes across as impatient for reform. Adamowski has fed a culture in which key administrators are willing to change course midyear if something isn't working. In short, there is a lot happening in Hartford and a lot to see. Test scores in the district have improved for three years running, with the latest 2009–2010 results showing students in grades 3–8 making improvements at twice the state average. It is too soon to know if Hartford has answers, but the district certainly has compelling ideas.

Because much of this work in Hartford is unfolding, and since re-sults—while appearing to move in the right direction—are far from final, the book includes two schools that offer longer views of turn-around. Located in Cincinnati, Ohio, Withrow University High School and Taft Information Technology High School began their dramatic reform efforts in 2001 under different federal pressures. These schools grappled with many of the same challenges urban turnaround schools struggle with today and, for that reason, their approaches are informa-tive. (I also focused on these schools because of their narrative connec-tion: Hartford superintendent Steven Adamowski was previously the superintendent of schools in Cincinnati and, in fact, hired the prin-cipals of both Withrow University and Taft as part of that city's high school redesign effort.)

These schools are also worth considering because they sustained im-provement over several years. They were low-performing schools and now they are high-performing schools. And, if you ask the principals at both schools, they will tell you that turnaround is not done yet. Taft, for example, is slated in December 2010 to move into a brand new building, which is spurring new initiatives, including plans to offer dinner (they al-ready provide breakfast and lunch) so that students from this high-pov-erty neighborhood will spend even more of their time benefiting from the safety and guidance available inside schoolhouse walls.

In addition to looking back on success stories, I have tried to look for-ward. As reform efforts evolve, there are strategies coming from high-performing charter school leaders like Knowledge Is Power Program (KIPP) and Achievement First, particularly around talent develop-ment, that are becoming increasingly relevant to district public schools. While research on charter schools overall shows mixed success, these particular organizations have recorded impressive results with students in high-poverty urban environments. These charters have evolved as they've worked in inner-city schools, and that process of learning and adjusting can inform turnaround work in other districts. In addition, they have paid particular attention to giving students in high-poverty schools access to social capital.

However turnaround is constructed, it must help students tap into a mind-set of achievement and offer them a vision of concrete goals that can seed motivation. In other words, they must understand why they must work hard at school—and, indeed, what working hard actually looks and feels like. The need to get students to understand the relevance of their classroom work to life opportunities is one reason schools can benefit from alliances with outside organizations and businesses. Hartford is doing this by assigning all schools a partner organization, and the Cincinnati schools have bona fide school-business partnerships, including Cincinnati Bell's corporate relationship with Taft.

And while many schools dream of strong bonds with big companies, there are also increasingly important relationships to be forged with nonprofits that can help in the actual work of turnaround. I report on a partnership between Garfield Middle School in Revere, Massachusetts, and the nonprofit Citizen Schools, which explicitly seeks to address the social capital gap with students as well as help the school address the need for academic and social support. (Disclosure: More than a decade ago, I volunteered to teach a journalism "apprenticeship" in Citizen Schools' summer program; the organization has changed a lot since then and no longer offers summer programs.) In examining Garfield Middle School's beginning efforts at turnaround, I touch on what I believe will be a lingering challenge: finding reform solutions and partners for high-poverty schools in small urban districts with few resources. These places need the support of programs like Citizen Schools because they don't have the staff, resources, or expertise of even moderate-size districts like Hartford. While large cities may attract nonprofit, foundation, and government dollars and attention for turnaround (after all, everyone wants a big, high-profile demonstration site to showcase their vision), there are thousands of smaller urban districts, like Revere, that must find some way to bring turnaround partners to their turf.

Finally, while this book includes reporting from schools spanning grades K–12, I have spent the most time in the high schools. I made this choice because the turnaround initiative comes at an especially key moment in high schoolers' lives. Whether dramatic reform succeeds or fails could well shape their immediate futures in starkly concrete ways, determining whether they struggle with poverty or find a road to financial and social stability. Will they graduate? Will they go to college? Or not? If revamped schools can engage and reorient students, helping them make dramatic academic gains and revealing new choices, that would be a stunning outcome. Yet, an ineffective high school turnaround can leave students unmoored and even questioning themselves. There is, after all, nothing robust about the social, academic, and economic supports for many of these students. Their futures are woven with thin threads. Turnaround has come at this moment and how well it works matters. A lot.

While this book uses narrative webs to examine the challenges schools in turnaround face, I have tried to structure it as simply as possible. The first chapter sets the policy and fiscal context for turnaround, explaining reasons for optimism and concern and hitting on the federal role in education. Chapter 2, "Why Johnny Needs a Rocket," gets at the achievement gap, focusing on the moral, political (including union), and social forces while considering how one district, Hartford, is structuring its work. The next chapter, "School-Level Lessons," offers an on-the-ground tour as principals and teachers try to take big ideas about turnaround and put them to work in their buildings. This chapter includes reporting from a principal and teachers who learn in September that their school will be closed at the end of the academic year.

"Suits, Cowboys, and Surrogate Moms," chapter 4, addresses school-level leadership by sharing very different approaches from particularly strong principals, both those in the midst of turnaround and those with a longer view. Chapter 5, "Teachers—the Very Front Line of Reform," considers the selection, development, and support of teachers who are

7

trying in a short span of time, and under increasing pressure, to change student expectations and performance. This chapter includes ideas from top-performing charter schools. For example, while early charter school wins depended heavily on heroic efforts and long hours of teachers, successful charter schools like Achievement First have made adjustments: for example, now tutors, not classroom teachers, work with students during Saturday sessions. This learning curve has yielded some thoughtful approaches to hiring and developing good teachers that may be useful to district school leaders in turnaround. The sixth chapter, "Partner, Network, Innovate," looks at how schools and districts are collaborating with both business and nonprofits in turnaround efforts. The final chapter, "There Is No Finish Line," considers strategies in sustaining performance once schools have reached targets. It frames challenges—How do you know if you are on the right track? What should goals and guideposts look like along the way?—and captures the unfortunate reality that steps toward success spawn new problems. Just because students get into college doesn't mean they can afford to go.

As a journalist, I believe in the power of eyewitness accounts and on-the-ground interviews to convey not just what *should* be happening but what *is* happening. For too long, schools in cities like Hartford were supposed to be educating students but weren't. Now they are trying—working quickly—to change all that. There is a lot of brainpower, money, and energy tied up in turnaround at this moment. For the sake of kids like those at the Law and Government Academy in Hartford, who now put on dress shoes to walk through the school's front doors, let's hope it yields results.

*   *   *

The Policy Distraction

There is no shortage of opinion on school turnaround. We hear that schools can't actually be turned around. Like stacking dishes or cards or blocks, we're told, just when it looks like you've turned a school around, built it up, and everything is balanced, some teeny, invisible shift of molecules in the air, or perhaps time or gravity, sends it crashing down. Test scores rise, and then they fall. People are excited about new ideas and new ways, and then those innovations feel stale and ineffective. Things stop working and return to how they were.

There are some, like Andy Smarick, distinguished visiting fellow at the Thomas B. Fordham Institute, who insist that schools that perform poorly will continue to perform poorly "despite being acted upon in innumerable ways." He also makes a rather tough, but noteworthy, point that, despite lots of studies and huge application of resources, no one knows how to make unsuccessful schools great. There are those who doubt this entire enterprise, who argue that the very idea of turning around failing schools won't work because there is too much baggage to overcome and because we don't have reliable ways to go about doing it. So, the argument goes, the only real way to address these troubled schools is to close them and start fresh with a new school.

As a policy argument, this makes a lot of sense. Schools are tightly constructed cultures where the people who run them are often deeply invested (sometimes even just by habit and not ideology) in preserving the rhythms and practices in place. If it is not working, how difficult is it to dismantle just the ineffective parts when we might not really understand which parts those are? If schools aren't working, some argue, they need a radical jolt. Shutting down and starting over certainly is radical. But here's the problem: reopened or new schools can be just as unsuccessful as those they replace. Will all of the new academies in Hartford Public High School be better than the old single high school? It's not clear. (In the course of reporting for this book, for example, district leaders decided to phase out one of the new academies.)

The imperative, then, is not closure and restart but a deeper exercise that involves reconsidering all the small pieces that constitute a schoolhouse—from how and what students learn to devising better approaches to engaging them, defining and managing school culture more carefully, rethinking how to hire and reward teachers, managing community and nonprofit partnerships more effectively, using data better, and coming up with more commonsense approaches to school discipline and academic struggles.

Taking scattershot aim at failed school turnarounds ignores the moment we're in: there is, for the first time in years, a broad consensus that we must actually dig in, understand why schools fail, and fix or replace them. There is today a more urgent conversation about educational disparities and a more vocal reminder that access to a quality education is a civil rights issue. While the passage of No Child Left Behind in 2001 framed education as a *civil* right, rather than just a right, there has never been broader agreement in the belief that the state's obligation is not merely promising a seat in a classroom but promising all students the tools, learning, and experiences that will actually educate them. This shift matters, because instead of seeing the student as solely responsible for engaging the education system, it is now the education system's job to engage the student.

This *is* a turnaround. Whether we close a school, open a new one, or fire the principal and replace the staff, the point is that schools must now engage students differently. The policy quest is an understandable eagerness to find what works and scale up. But for education leaders, principals, teachers, and others, the temptation to eye every creative solution as a potential scale-up can be a distraction. What works in one school for one population may not fly in another. If there is one thing that twenty-plus years reporting on schools has shown me, it is that each school is unique. That is not to say there aren't particular approaches and knowledge worth sharing, but it is essential to know your school and understand what works *there*. So, while scale matters to policy makers, daily school success is what matters to kids.

In fact, Richard Elmore makes this very point when he observes in an article in the January/February 2010 issue of the *Harvard Education Letter* that he "used to think that policy was the solution. And now I think that policy is the problem." The danger of policy innovation overload is very real. Every day as he works with teachers and administrators in schools, Elmore sees "the effects of a policy system that has run amok. There is no political discipline among elected officials and their advisers. To policy makers, every idea about what schools should be doing is as credible as every other idea, and any new idea that can command a political constituency can be used as an excuse for telling schools to do something."

This may be a risky point to make in a book offering ideas from inside school turnaround, but it is meant to calibrate the conversation about fixing schools. It is not clear what works everywhere. Hopefully, in some number of years we will know more than we do now.

Federal Money at the Margin

If, as Elmore says, the policy makers have run amok, at least they are doing it with some money attached. The federal push for school turnaround—demonstrated with $4.35 billion in Race to the Top funding, another $3.5 billion in Title I funding specifically for turnaround, and $650 million in i3 (Investing in Innovation) money—has been all about competitive grants. While this sounds like a lot of money, it is a small portion of the $100 billion allotted to education through the American Reinvestment and Recovery Act stimulus package. But, more pointedly, it represents a very small portion of the money actually spent on K–12 public education. In the 2006–2007 school year, for example, figures from the National Center for Education Statistics show federal money accounted for just 8.5 percent of school revenues. (That is dramatically more than in, say, 1919–1920 when the federal government provided just 0.3 percent but less than in the late 1970s when federal money made up as much as 9.8 percent of school revenues.)

While federal dollars comprise a small slice of school budgets, however, it represents money at the margin. Unlike local tax and other school revenues that cover things like building maintenance, basic salaries, insurance, and supplies, this new federal money can help a school rethink what it provides its students. The particular challenge is that the pressure to innovate (and win federal dollars) comes as local and state budgets are strained and as districts are forced to make cuts, in some cases laying off large numbers of teachers. So while the feds—and Secretary of Education Arne Duncan in particular—have been taken with the neat bit of leverage that has come with competitive grants, the on-the-ground economic pressures lead some districts to work at cross-purposes. It's tough to innovate and then lay off the very teachers who have just been trained to carry out new initiatives because they lack seniority. The goal for education leaders is to have a cohesive turnaround vision and find funding to power the work (as opposed to being lured into doing work because particular dollars are available, regardless of how it fits the plan). This is a rather obvious point, but, amid so much change, leaders need to stay focused and, where possible, find creative ways to use the system to gain needed support for their work.

This is not to say the federal education agenda has not been important in getting states and districts to consider fresh approaches. After all, in the months after the funding requirements were announced, state legislatures were busy raising legal limits on charter schools, dropping firewalls barring use of student data to judge teacher performance, and developing common standards in math and language arts—all at one point conditions of seeking federal money (some rules have since changed). The federal agenda has also articulated priorities that have given a framework and language to district efforts. For example, the federal push to take thirty-eight education funding streams and consolidate them into eleven programs representing key focus areas helps clarify the education agenda. By deciding what matters most, states and districts can set goals likely to have traction, research grounding, and to gain financial support. Still broad in scope, they do provide guideposts. Included among the focus areas described in the Federal Register are: (1) college and career readiness; (2) teachers and leaders; (3) well-rounded education, including not just math and reading but also history, science, technology/engineering, math, and the arts; (4) support for student success, including safer schools and "thinking about extended learning time"; (5) emphasis on innovation; (6) recognition of diverse student needs, including migrant and homeless students and English language learners.

For districts seeking to turn around failing schools, the largest chunk of federal money is distributed as School Improvement Grants; by contrast, only fifty out of 500 points in the Race to the Top scoring system are explicitly awarded for turning around the lowest-performing schools. And where most Race to the Top money goes to states, which get to keep 50 percent of the award and subgrant the rest to districts, 95 percent of School Improvement Grants must go directly to districts and schools (the state can take only 5 percent to administer the grant). This turnaround money supports four "interventions" by now familiar to education leaders. This is how the Department of Education describes them:

- *Turnaround model:* This would include, among other actions, replacing the principal and at least 50 percent of the school's staff, adopting a new governance structure, and implementing a new or revised instructional program.
- *Restart model:* School districts would close failing schools and reopen them under the management of a charter school operator, a charter management organization, or an educational management organization selected through a rigorous review process. A restart school would be required to admit, within the grades it serves, any former student who wishes to attend.
- *School closure:* The district would close a failing school and enroll the students who attended that school in other high-achieving schools in the district.
- *Transformational model:* Districts would address four specific areas: (1) developing teacher and school leader effectiveness, which includes replacing the principal who led the school prior to commencement of the transformational model; (2) implementing comprehensive instructional reform strategies; (3) extending learning and teacher planning time and creating community-oriented schools; and (4) providing operating flexibility and sustained support.

Clearly, the transformational model is the least dramatic and school closure is the most extreme. The government wants schools and districts to choose what works best for them but does not want all turnarounds to follow the same recipe. In seeking School Improvement Grant money, districts are required to identify schools as Tier 1, Tier 2, or Tier 3 (with Tier 1 as the lowest-achieving 5 percent of Title I schools in the state) but demands that "any district with nine or more schools in school improvement will not be allowed to use any single strategy in more than half of its schools," according to an August 2009 Education Department press release (and spelled out in the grant application guidelines as well). In other words, the goal is for districts to come up with a variety of fixes aimed at helping schools at different grade levels that are facing different degrees of failure. It is not merely to find solutions for the most troubled schools but to also seek corrections for faltering schools before they become a district's or state's lowest performers.

The federal agenda, then, is about offering key help as well as about pushing for fresh thinking that can be applied in the future. The government wants new ideas for the worst schools but also solid intervention for schools that may not be as badly off track—and it wants cooperation and information sharing among districts and at the state level. In other words, the results of innovation—Did it work or not?—need to be shared. And because gathering such information as well as directing interventions is a big job, schools and districts will need to (and want to) partner with outside organizations. Some of these will be nonprofit educational support organizations or community groups that can both help get these federal and other private funds (thereby paying for their services) as well as do work that districts can't do on their own. This can range from actually structuring and guiding turnaround to addressing social needs that affect a child's in-school success. It may be a departure from past practice to rely increasingly on outsiders, but there is more to do than districts can handle themselves.

Andrew Calkins, now a senior program officer at the Stupsky Foundation, was formerly at Mass Insight and is one of the authors of a key Bill and Melinda Gates Foundation–funded report, *The Turnaround Challenge*, which set out important thinking about the preconditions and structure of turnaround. Calkins said in an interview that while this influx of federal money presents opportunity for districts, it also represents a danger. "There is nothing to stop every professional development company from slapping a turnaround label on their door." Ironically, he tells about when he and his colleagues were preparing *The Turnaround Challenge:* "we were hoping there would be a real boost in federal support for school improvement and that it would be four or five years down the road. Now all of that money will be poured into the turnaround sector before it's ready. We are at risk of making the mistake of trying to do the scale up before we know what the work looks like."

The Drama of Reform

It seems odd for Calkins to suggest that anyone in education would be afraid of money, especially a lot of money, but his caution is important. This so-called once-in-a-lifetime infusion of cash into school reform and turnaround tests the judgment of education leaders. If several years from now the effort is summed up as an ineffective spending spree, there may be no political will to adequately fund education, never mind education innovation. However, if this truly does yield results that ripple beyond test scores to graduation rates, college completion, economic security, and a more globally competitive workforce, well, then, education spending may just look like the bargain its advocates have been claiming it is.

While spending and funding arguments have been the province of policy makers, education secretary Arne Duncan has infused the competition for federal dollars with all the drama of the Academy Awards. This is not a bad thing. When the first round of sixteen finalists for

Race to the Top funds were announced at 11:30 A.M. on Thursday, March 4, 2010, it set off elation and disappointment among the forty states and the District of Columbia that had applied. A few states—including Texas—made a show of not seeking the money, arguing that federal demands interfered with state education autonomy. Despite some grumbling, most states have responded to Secretary Duncan's pass-the-envelope-please approach and have played along.

It's worth noting that reports of the March 4 announcement represented the first time in recent memory that most people had ever *heard* or *cared* that a state application for federal money had made it through the first level and to the final round of reviews (or not). School reform has, in other words, become news. In California, March 4, 2010, became a day of statewide walkouts, passionate demonstrations, and protests about expected education cuts once the state was shut out in the first round of Race to the Top funding. While the scene was generally peaceful, the *Los Angeles Times* did report some violence, including a broken windshield, pulled fire alarms, and demonstrators forcing authorities to close Oakland's I-880 at rush hour.

Large public protests over education funding?

This is a changed landscape. Education reform, often mired in insider jargon, is now a matter of public interest and discussion. School leaders must realize that while they may be experts on the matter, they must craft arguments that invite public support and scrutiny. As a long-term strategy, this can only increase public involvement in education and make apparent that we all have a stake in what goes on in the nation's schools.

When Will We Get There?

Ironically, despite federal prescriptions and requirements about school reform approaches, there is little guidance about what turnaround actually means. How do you know when you get there? Schools that appear successful one year may look lackluster a year or two later. How will turnaround be defined, particularly since proficiency levels and the difficulty of tests vary widely from state to state?

We are moving to a standard of success that looks more to measuring progress than to giving a thumbs-up/-down of who has passed or failed. This is reasonable considering that many children in high-poverty urban schools are one or more years behind grade level in reading and math. Figuring out how to help them advance, say 1.5 years' worth of learning in one school year, is useful and probably says more about how well, say, a new literacy strategy is working than comparing year-to-year test failure percentages. This will require better measures that track cohorts. Increasingly, the goal is a comparative one: closing the achievement gap. Helping every child have access to the academic tools and support to achieve at the same level as the most privileged is a tangible and useful goal, particularly if we can get the standards right and compare them internationally. Progress, after all, is about reaching for some worthwhile finish line.

Measures of progress—together with other data such as graduation rates, attendance, dropout rates, parent attendance at conferences—matter when it comes to figuring out if turnaround is successful. But in the rush (and one of the things characteristic of this moment in education reform history is the frenzied energy of those on the front lines), we must not forget the power of the less tangible qualities of education, including helping poor children see what they can do and be.

At the Dr. Ramon E. Betances School in Hartford, a school slated for closure several months after my visit, I spoke with a group of fourth and fifth graders. One of the girls, Asura, clearly relished the conversation and had to be reminded now and again to let other children finish their sentences. But as I listened to this radiant girl who played baseball with boys and seemed to have an opinion on everything, I couldn't help but see what a dynamo she was. I often ask children what they want to do when they grow up, and while Asura was quick to help Celia, who couldn't decide between being an artist and a zookeeper ("You could do both. You could be a painter that paints animals!"), she was oddly unimaginative about her own future. She said she wanted to go to college so that she could get a job in the grocery department at B.J.'s Wholesale Club, like her grandmother.

When I pressed her—What would you really like to do if you could do *anything in the world?*—she was quiet. Her dream job? "I was thinking of working at a Nike store, helping people pick out what kind of sneakers they want," she said.

I understand that career ideas change as children age. The child who at two wants to drive a garbage truck and work the smasher at five plans to be a starting quarterback in the NFL and at ten thinks it would be cool to be a scientist. Children need an identity; their dreams provide purpose and a sense of self on a daily basis. And so while goals change, we must help children compose a sense of possibility for themselves. Otherwise, why do the math problem, why study for the history test?

Sadly, Asura's response was not unique. I have had so many conversations with bright children in urban schools who do not know what they are working for or how the world of college and jobs and opportunities actually works. They are savvy about some things but profoundly insecure about others. I have spoken to students in guidance offices strewn with college flags who have applied to colleges and utter names of places they want to attend, but, when I draw them out, they admit they have no honest understanding of what one really *does* at college. They look tough but are vulnerable and terrified of being told they don't belong. Even when they make it to college, even when they are sitting in classes, their internal voice tells them everyone else is better. Too many never graduate—not because they couldn't, but because they don't believe that they actually can. They take themselves out of contention for things they could achieve because they feel as if they are standing on the edge of a cliff and have no ability to guess if they will fall or fly.

Failure, especially repeated failure—even if it is not your own but is all around you—is painful. Altering the coefficients in this stubborn equation is the huge, unmeasured job of education reform. In whatever language we evoke, whether rooted in social justice or civil rights or international competitiveness, the work of changing the factors that keep poor urban children from the life opportunities experienced by their wealthier suburban peers forms the energetic core of the hope so many have for school turnaround. This is about far more than a government program.

2

WHY JOHNNY NEEDS A ROCKET

HARTFORD PUBLIC HIGH SCHOOL, the nation's second-oldest secondary school which once prepared young men for Ivy League educations, now sits among check-cashing stores and laundromats in a neighborhood that lies in the shadow of Interstate 84's concrete musculature, which whisks most of the world past the city blight and out to Connecticut's charming towns with their public greens, white churches, and, yes, really good schools.

That contrast—poor cities, rich suburbs—is at the heart of the disparity between whites' and minorities' educational outcomes, access to quality jobs, health care, and even life expectancy and cancer death rates. Like inner cities across America, Hartford has collected the poor: nearly one-third of its residents live below the poverty line. Depending on which census figures you consider, Hartford is one of the nation's poorest cities located in the nation's second-richest state. And according to data from the National Assessment of Educational Progress, the "Nation's Report Card," Connecticut is home to the largest achievement gap between poor and nonpoor pupils in the United States.

Despite this dubious status, Hartford's education story is, in many ways, America's education story. After decades of rock-bottom test scores, high dropout rates, dangerous schools, and a sense that this was a normal state of affairs, the district is trying to turn things around. In November 2006, the city hired as its school superintendent Steven Adamowski, a Connecticut native who led a school reform movement in Cincinnati and who speaks of educational disparities as "the biggest civil rights issue since the passage of the voting rights act."

The Moral Mission

Steven Adamowski is obviously not the only one to describe the problem of failing schools as a civil rights issue. This idea is at the spiritual heart of reform—and reform not solely from the federal government down but from the grassroots, individual-teacher, nonprofit foundation, entrepreneurial, fix-the-world philanthropy on up. This is social change in the moment, a cause that is drawing a stunning array of smart and motivated young people into education who in another era might have been lured by investment banks and consulting firms, maybe even cool business start-ups.

As a result, there is a particular vibe around urban school reform not unlike the passion of the organic farming and foodie movement. Only instead of handmade, batch-grown, and slow-made, the quest for results is urgent. Both, however, share an intense care, a dig-in-and-do-it-right ethos, an it's-bigger-than-me sensibility. When I asked Dacia Toll—Rhodes Scholar and Yale Law School grad who helped start Amistad Academy, a charter school in New Haven, Connecticut, that has evolved into the Achievement First network—how their teacher hiring was different from the way districts do it, she was stumped. "This is all I've ever known," she said.

The power of smart people who did not come up through the system thinking about how to help Johnny (grade levels behind in reading and math) not only catch up but also prepare for college and learn the social skills to operate in middle-class America makes this an extremely compelling moment. The fact that the federal government has jumped on top of the pile feeds an adrenaline-charged rush of reform that is both exciting and exhausting to watch. This is why we must figure out what works: to inject sanity and sustainability into radical school reform.

Education people are not used to having so much support align behind them and a specific goal—in this case, closing the achievement gap. This does not mean there's no debate about why or how to fix the problem of poor kids performing poorly. For years there has been a fault line in education reform around how to get at the root of the matter. If societal problems like poverty, violence, drugs, mental health issues make it impossible for children in these communities to succeed in school, shouldn't we fix those social issues first? Flooding schools with innovative ideas will yield little if the deepest problems are outside the building. Others disagree, arguing that if we take a wide-armed approach, fixing schools will, eventually, address the social problems that keep children from achieving. Important work can happen, they argue, even in a broken social environment.

This is the belief that informs turnaround work. James S. Coleman's equality of educational opportunity study, commissioned in 1966 by the U.S. Department of Health, Education and Welfare, and best known simply as the Coleman Report, made clear the connections between home advantage and school success. That finding has been explored in many studies since, linking school achievement with various aspects of a student's home environment, from socioeconomic status to mother's education level to the quality of vocabulary used in daily conversation. Rather than serving as an explanation for poor performance of some pupils, this research is being interpreted as a reason to reach deeper and wider. "You have to have schools that are so robust, that 80 to 90 percent of achievement can come from the school," says Adamowski, who likes to say that schools are a tool to "break the cultural bonds of poverty" in Hartford.

Joe Nathan, director of the Center for School Change at Macalester College, embraces the civil rights mantra of education reform. He points out that his mother, Ruth K. Nathan, opened one of the first fifty Head Start programs in the country in Wichita, Kansas, in

1965. He believes schools can act in ways such that change can ripple outside of classrooms and reshape student outcomes, which is why he, with Gates Foundation funding, got involved in guiding high school restructuring in Cincinnati in 2001.

In his view, what made the work possible was that in May 2000 a school board committee issued a report, "High School Restructuring," that affirmed that the district's aim was not to go through the motions of reform and chop big schools into smaller ones (the vogue at the moment) but to figure out how to design schools to raise achievement for inner-city kids. Says Nathan, "They decided that changes in the high schools didn't have to wait until there was less racism."

Two schools, Withrow University High School and Taft Information Technology High School, have made noteworthy gains and sustained them. Interestingly, while the schools' two principals have different approaches and personal styles, Nathan says they have both expressed to him "that they have some spiritual sense that this is what they are supposed to be doing."

Good people are signing on for the mission—not just for careers in education but in *urban* education—because they want to have an impact. "I wanted to work with children in an urban setting," said a thirty-three-year-old Hartford elementary school principal. "I wanted to be a person who could instill in them, 'You have a future.' I know it sounds clichéd, but I do want to be a part of it."

Closing the achievement gap, then, is a test result target as well as a goal with social and cultural aspirations. It's nice to have a feel-good aspect to what is really very hard work, but what do you actually need to do? What is the unit of reform? There may be big talk in Washington and at think tanks, but how does this play out on the ground? Reform efforts thus far have not been organized or orderly. They have relied heavily on talented and motivated individuals to drive transformation in compartmentalized areas, often geographically or programmatically. There are stories of promising programs and schools defying odds to produce results.

Such isolated victories cannot drive widespread and lasting reform, says Alex Johnston, CEO of the education advocacy group ConnCAN (Connecticut Coalition for Achievement Now) who also serves on the New Haven board of education and on a state commission developing a preK–20 data system. (He's also a Rhodes Scholar.) "While there really is no one single reform that will transform a district, the vital unit of change *is* the district," he says one morning at ConnCAN's New Haven office, whose sparse décor and abundance of pamphlets suggest a campaign headquarters. "It is not until a district embraces [dramatic] change that we are likely to see sustained turnaround. What you will see [otherwise] are pockets of excellence where a strong leader by force of personality will bring together teachers and you will see a success story."

Expectations and Consequences

It is too early to know if the Hartford Public School District, which serves more than 22,000 children, will be a success story worth talking about in several years, but early work appears promising. Superintendent Steven Adamowski is employing a portfolio approach to district management, giving families options that include charter-operated, Montessori, traditional district, and magnet schools as well as theme-based science and language academies (an Asian Studies Academy is to open in 2010–2011) and career-focused high schools. While the Connecticut State Supreme Court's 1996 decision in Sheff v. O'Neil spurred on creation of interdistrict magnet schools as part of a mandated desegregation plan that would bring students from twenty-seven area towns into the city schools, those magnets are managed as part of the Hartford Public School System (although funded differently, only partly through direct state per-pupil appropriation).

The purpose of essentially branding all the schools as part of a single system, says Adamowski, "is to avoid what we had in the past; high-end magnets [for parents who knew the system]—and then the majority of city schools where everyone else went." One reality that complicates reform is that urban districts have "education choosers," inner-city parents who may be poor but are involved and invested in their children's educations. These parents are savvy about which schools are top performers and how to get spots in them, leaving less able families to the less desirable choices. While charter schools have lottery systems so that admission appears random, it is common for parents of students seeking seats to be required to attend informational meetings and otherwise demonstrate a commitment in order to *even enter the lottery*. The filtering process can get even more subtle, as one former magnet school administrator explained: "I was in conversations where we said, 'We will make our brochures with lots and lots of words so some families will be overwhelmed with all the words and they won't send their kids.'"

Issues, then, are not just of access but also of parent motivation and information. One troubling fact to come from No Child Left Behind is that while the ability of parents to switch their children out of troubled schools was touted as a key, revolutionary feature, studies show that few parents use this option. A 2009 Rand report prepared for the U.S. Department of Education on state and local implementation of NCLB noted that in the 2006–2007 school year, less than 1 percent of those eligible transferred to better schools. This and other studies show that when students actually do transfer, they typically move to other poor and low-performing schools.

To middle-class parents who spend a lot of time thinking about their child's educational pathway, this seems puzzling. But Alex Johnston, who before heading ConnCAN was part of the management team that turned around the New Haven Housing Authority and helped it avoid receivership, said that in public housing, "anybody who could get out, did get out, leaving a greater concentration of people with real challenges." In education, he says, there is the often-posed question, "What happens to the parents who don't have the capacity to exercise choice?" If reform is "done right" insists Johnston, in relentlessly closing schools for chronically low performance "you break up places where students might become clustered" and, of course, acclimated to a culture of failure. (Research also suggests that parents whose children are in failing schools are satisfied with the teaching.)

When Adamowski arrived in Hartford, twenty-eight schools (out of a total of thirty-nine) were, he says, "so god awful, the only way I can describe it is if you were in high school or college and taking tests and you never performed above a 50." The cohort graduation rate (how many kids who started high school earned a diploma) was 29 percent. Between the fall of 2007 and the fall of 2009, Hartford opened sixteen new schools and closed seven for low performance. In the Hartford Public High School building, for example, the district closed one school and opened four. In preparation for the 2010–2011 school year, four schools were "redesigned," Hartford's term for shutting down, rethinking structure and personnel, and hiring a new principal (who, in turn, hires staff and trains them in time to open in September).

The theme of closure, redesign, and restart is a familiar cycle in Hartford. For example, Adamowski sips his green tea during an interview in his office located on the eighth floor of an art deco–style building that was once the flagship home of the Hartford-based G. Fox Department Store, the national retailer that went bankrupt in the 1990s. Today it is predominantly office and retail space, though like a lot of the city a good deal of that space goes unrented (one reason why new schools have not struggled to find space). Adamowski also exemplifies a personal restart, making a point of saying that he was a poor student until his junior year in college, when he effectively turned himself around and discovered a passion for education.

As superintendent, Adamowski has been both critiqued and praised by ConnCAN and vilified by the teacher union. In an hour-long interview, Hartford Federation of Teachers president Andrea Johnson does not utter Adamowski's name once, referring to him only as "this superintendent." ConnCAN, however, which tracks testing data for every school in the state and makes it available on the group's Web site, notes that Hartford has made the greatest gains on state tests of any Connecticut city over the past two years, and new data suggests that Hartford again made the largest gains.

One critical piece of Hartford's approach is student-based budgeting. "We fund the child as opposed to the school," says Adamowski. This means that instead of making an annual per-pupil allocation to schools based on their size, dollars are tied to the specific student with the total determined by adding a student's *need weight* to the *grade weight.* For example, grade weights set a basic per-pupil expenditure for preK at $6,000; kindergarten at $5,551; grades 1–3 at $7,779; 4–6 at $6,483; grades 7 and 8 at $7,132; and grades 9–12 at $8,428. Then schools receive additional money depending on a student's needs, ranging from how much academic intervention they require (as much as $627 extra) to their progress as English language learners (as much as $2,593 extra for those studying English for fewer than thirty months) and special education (levels 1 to 4, ranging from $4,678 to $23,735 extra). While Adamowski recognizes that parents generally want children to attend schools near their homes, this approach feeds consumer-style competition among schools. This, in turn, changes the relationship of the parent to the school administrators. Schools that don't attract students will lose funding and could be closed or otherwise recast.

In describing the district's relationship to its schools, Adamowski refers to a color-coded performance matrix that has become the visual image of turnaround in the district (see tables 2.1 and 2.2). The broad idea of what he calls "managed performance" is similar to what the federal government has proposed in its reauthorization of the Elementary and Secondary Education Act: do a good job and get more freedom; struggle and face oversight or intervention.

In Hartford schools are judged on both their overall performance and their rate of improvement. On the double-axis matrix, schools at the bottom right, in red (dark gray), face intervention, which typically means closure and redesign by the district office. Those at the top left, in a spring green (medium gray), are *autonomous,* face less district interference, and earn their principals, teachers, and staff cash bonuses.

(Schools not in the very top performance category but making steady improvement may also have autonomous status). In between the top and bottom is *defined autonomy* in yellow (light gray), which reflects degrees of district involvement. New schools get three years to make gains. Struggling schools get two years to right themselves or face redesign. The goal is a four percentage point per year rate of improvement in the city's overall school improvement (OSI) metric, which correlates to student performance on state tests.

The magic number is an OSI of 70 or greater, which roughly means that most students in the school are performing at "proficient" or higher (the state's five levels are below basic, basic, proficient, goal, and advanced) on state tests, including math, reading, and writing. Most schools are below—and some even far below—this target. In the 2009–2010 school year, five schools reached an OSI of 70 or greater, and four of them were magnets (Dwight Elementary School was the only nonmagnet to make the target). Adamowski says that while improvement—even dramatic school change—can happen right away, it will take several years to get Hartford students on an academic plane with rest of the state. "If the lowest-performing school were to continuously improve at 4 percent, we would close the achievement gap in eight years," he says, noting that the state as a whole has been improving at a rate of about 1 percent per year of students reaching "proficient" or above on state tests. "In order to close the achievement gap, we have to quadruple the rate of state growth."

While it all sounds very orderly, albeit challenging, reality is messier. A new, promising school ends up with a principal who isn't right and is replaced. At another building that now houses several schools, there are so many entrances that it is hard to keep track of students as they wander from school to school. News of school closures can be clumsy, making surprised staff irate. Principals spend time figuring out ways to get around teacher union rules or grab the best teachers first. And, of course, the worst performing schools do *not* improve at a rate of 4 percent per year; some actually lose ground and perform worse than they did the previous year. These are just a few complications.

Table 2.1 2009–2010 school performance matrix based on 2009 results of CMT and CAPT

	2008–2009 RATE OF IMPROVEMENT				Baseline year New and redesigned schools
	Improving > = +4.0	Maintaining +3.9 to –3.9	Declining < = –4		
RELATIVE Goal range: OSI 70+	University High Dwight	Hartford Magnet Middle Classical Capital Preparatory		*Autonomous*	
PERFORO Proficient: OSI 50 to 69	Parkville Kinsella Kennelly Wish Fisher Simpson-Waverly M.L. King	Sport and Medical Sciences Webster Breakthrough Pathways Hooker Naylor Rawson West Middle Batchelder			Achievement First Hartford Global Communications/IB
RMANCE Below proficient: OSI below 50	Clark Quirk Middle	Moylan Burr Sanchez McDonough Bellizzi Middle Betances	Weaver 10–12	*Intervention/redesign*	M.D. Fox CommPACT Bulkeley Lower HPHS—Law and Government HPHS—Nursing Burns Latino Studies HPHS—Engineering and Green Technology Milner Core Knowledge Culinary Arts

New and redesigned schools 2009–2010
America's Choice at S.A.N.D.
Breakthrough II
High School, Inc.
Journalism and Media High School
Montessori
OPPortunity High School

Note: Schools not consisting of a grade that participates in the CMT or CAPT : Bulkeley Upper, HPHS Freshman Academy

Table 2.2 2010–2011 school performance matrix based on 2010 results of CMT and CAPT

		2009–2010 RATE OF IMPROVEMENT			Baseline year New and redesigned schools defined autonomy
RELATIVE PERFORMANCE		Improving >= +4.0	Maintaining +3.9 to -3.9	Declining <= -4	
Goal range: OSI 70+	Autonomous	Hartford Magnet Middle Classical Magnet Webster* Sport and Medical Sciences Breakthrough Magnet Achievement First Hartford	University High Capital Preparatory Magnet Parkville* Dwight		Montessori Magnet at Fisher
Proficient: OSI 50 to 69		Kinsella Fisher* Global Communications/IB Burr Bulkeley Lower M.L. King* Sanchez McDonough	Wish* Hooker Pathways Kennelly* Rawson* Naylor West Middle		America's Choice at S.A.N.D.*
Below proficient: OSI below 50	Intervention/redesign	HPHS—Nursing Betances HPHS—Law and Government Culinary Arts HPHS—Academic English and green technology Burns Latino Studies Milner Core Knowledge*	M.D. Fox CommPACT* Moylan* Batchelder* J.C. Clark* Bellizzi Quirk Middle	Simpson-Waverly*	High School, Inc. Weaver Journalism and Media Breakthrough II OPportunityHigh School

New & Redesigned Schools 2010–2011
Annie Fisher STEM School
Asian Studies Dwight/Bellizzi
Betances Early Reading Lab School
Rawson Middle Grades Academy

*Results for Renzulli Academy students reflected in sending schools, OSI at Goal (89)

Note: Schools not consisting of a grade that participates in the CMT or CAPT: Bulkeley Upper, HPHS Freshman Academy, Weaver 11–12

What is striking about Hartford, however, is the pragmatism of Adamowski's team. The system is not brittle and takes reworking on the fly. Joan Massey, assistant superintendent for secondary schools, has a thumb ring on her right hand and carries a plastic leopard bag stuffed with multicolored folders as she makes her school rounds. This Hartford native may as well be the poster child for Hartford turnaround. "My personal style is more of rip the Band Aid off and really dig into all the reform," she says, sipping on a Dunkin Donuts regular with cream. "I understand there are people who move in this slow and steady and organized way, but the results matter to me. I always look at everything as a time crunch." Massey says she signed on to the agenda in Hartford because, after years of watching—sometimes from afar (she worked in Seattle)—she had a belief that Adamowski's turnaround vision could be for real: "I thought this might be a person who might actually help transform Hartford—finally."

Substance and Style: How Hartford Designs a School

One of the things Adamowski brought to Hartford was the belief that good schools didn't just happen—you had to design them to work. This philosophy has its roots in the Bush-era quest (yes, through competitive grant funding) for a "new generation of American schools" founded on research-based practices with effective teaching and learning that were mutually reinforcing. It all fit together like a puzzle. This wasn't about a better pullout program for disadvantaged students, about phonics versus whole language; instead it was about integrated, layered, enmeshed "whole school reform." And at the center of this was the design, which was another way of saying that a number of key strategies were all lined up to work together. These include the same things we seek today in effective schools: a school structure organized to focus on teaching and learning (teacher leadership teams, collaboration, shared responsibility for student success, smart scheduling); college and career-ready curriculum and instruction that is project based and engaging; academic and social support for students; increased teacher and principal effectiveness (professional learning communities, collaboration, relevant professional development, including working with data); partnership with other schools, community organizations, and educational institutions; the building of a school culture of continuous improvement.

In Hartford, the person in charge of this work is Christina Kishimoto, assistant superintendent of school design. She is a petite, energetic woman who projects a no-nonsense demeanor and does not shy from tough conversations. As with Joan Massey, the education-emergency quality of Hartford's turnaround effort seems to suit her style. She points out that when she makes demands—urging principals, for instance, to do a better job of marketing their schools and print brochures to hand out to parents attending the citywide school choice fair—some complain they lack money in the budget. "Whenever people say, 'There's a cost to that,' I say, 'figure out what's not working. Stop doing it and there are your funds.' If you do five or six pizza parties a year to bring parents in, stop doing them if you have five people show up to each of these parties. Use that money to do your brochures."

Because the design process is intertwined with school performance, Kishimoto spends a lot of time with Adamowski's color-coded matrix. She uses it to track which schools are improving enough in their OSI rating to jump categories as well as which schools are remaining static and which are struggling, perhaps even falling into an area that calls for district intervention. Newly redesigned schools get a fresh start and a year in which they do not have an OSI rating. After that, it's a push for that 4 percent improvement and a quest for an OSI of 70.

What Hartford calls *redesign* is what Secretary of Education Arne Duncan calls *turnaround*. It is dramatic, but it's not the district's only approach to school turnaround. In what would be listed as *restart* in the Duncan dictionary would in Hartford be the district inviting, for example, the charter network Achievement First to open elementary and middle schools in August 2008 (while now K–2 and grades 5 and 6, the school will eventually span K–8). And, rather than waiting for schools to need redesign, Kishimoto considers which schools may need some extra district help in the form of intervention teams, which work with school-based teams to provide extra curriculum and instructional support and coaching. At the same time some schools are redesigned, Hartford is also trying to create more K–8 schools, a move that shapes some decision making. "Parents don't like middle schools," says Kishimoto. For example, the top-performing Dwight Elementary School, located in one of the city's oldest school buildings that is not up to current standards, was recently merged with the struggling Bellizzi Middle School to form the new Dwight-Bellizzi Asian Studies Academy, which has been located in the renovated Bellizzi Middle School building. The Asian Studies Academy, says Kishimoto, "will equip students with a more global affairs education." And, because the school will emphasize Mandarin language (all teachers must take an introductory course, and ten were sent to summer immersion programs in China in summer 2010, with others to follow in 2011), Kishimoto says many of the students who are now native Spanish speakers will pick up a third language.

Redesign, however, is at the heart of the districtwide turnaround effort, and, accordingly, there is an established cycle of planning, design, and school openings. New school design specifications are in place the December prior to reopening. The new principal is hired in February. The principal hires staff in April. Over the spring and summer the school is retrofitted to the theme, and curriculum and staff training takes place. The school opens in August. While Kishimoto uses the academic year to manage this process and support newly opened schools, she spends the summer fleshing out ideas for new school designs. She presents initial designs to the board of education for feedback and, in some cases, approval. Approved designs go back to the design team for more research and formulation of more detailed plans (that ultimately go back to the board for review and adoption). Some conversations with the board are about creating coherent pathways for students. "We know with the development of a K–8 language school [the Dwight-Bellizzi Asian Studies Academy and a Latino Studies Academy at Burns Elementary], we know we need to finish it off with a high school," says Kishimoto. Likewise, she says, the board is "very committed to a preK–12 Montessori."

Ideas for new schools come mostly from established national models, but some are homegrown based on community wants. The district has designed schools around America's Choice, Core Knowledge, Montessori, and International Baccalaureate and used the National Academy Foundation model for math to create the Academy of Engineering and Green Technology. For the Law and Government Academy, Kishimoto says they created a design that is a composite of a number of law-focused academy school designs. The Culinary Arts Academy evolved from a state department of education plan.

The district design team has created its own models for schools, such as Breakthrough II, an attempt to replicate Breakthrough Magnet, which originally started as charter school. Likewise, Kishimoto says, the language-based academy models were developed in-house. The Burns Latino Studies Academy in particular, she says, was developed by her team in response to parents at the former Burns Elementary, which was closed and redesigned into a preK–8, who wanted a school that recognized and supported their culture. "As part of redesign, the students remain," says Kishimoto. "We are not looking for parents to leave their neighborhood school, so we want a model that is attractive to them."

The school design provides school leaders with the organizing principles for running the school. The design may include details about course offerings, extracurricular offerings, the length of the school day, and even how teachers will work together. In Hartford, uniforms are also part of school redesign (every school, redesigned or not, has a uniform). At the elementary level, they tend to be simple: typically white shirts and khaki pants or jumpers. At the high schools, particularly career-focused academies, uniforms reflect a vocational bent. For example, nursing students wear scrubs (seniors get to wear white lab coats, too), and Law and Government Academy students wear white dress shirts, black and white striped ties, blazers or V-neck sweaters with the LGA logo, black slacks, and dress shoes.

Each redesigned school also has a community partner, and these partners typically serve as part of the school's design team and are meant to help schools keep their offerings relevant and up-to-date. Some even offer key funding. Travelers Insurance, for example, led a group of insurance and financial industry partners to put up $750,000 to aid the 2009–2010 academic year opening of High School, Inc., a business-focused high school. The companies also serve on the school's advisory board and have committed to providing up to seventy paid internships each year to the school's seniors. The University of Connecticut Medical Center and Capitol Community College have partnered with the nursing academy. Some students take classes at the community college, and the high school serves as a feeder to both institutions' nursing programs.

Poor performance is the primary trigger for school redesign. In the case of Bulkeley High School (pronounced *Buckley*), Kishimoto says that the school's failure to make academic progress, plus its large size— 1,600 students—and behavior problems, spurred her to divide the school into a lower school and an upper school. "We just couldn't let it run as it was running," says Kishimoto, noting that a large proportion of students were several grade levels behind in reading. "Close to half needed intensive academic intervention; that's a large number of students, 300 or 400 students." There were also fights outside the school and disorder in the hallways. Kishimoto had the lower school focus on helping students earn enough credits to be promoted. The upper grades were made into two academies, a teacher prep academy and a humanities academy, which opened in 2010. While this sort of restructuring "looks a lot like redesign," admits Kishimoto, instead of the district driving the changes, she sends in district coaches for support but creates a school-based team "to empower the existing staff to turn around their own school."

And as for behavior problems, including kids ganging up on one another and "tagging up the hallways and stairwell" with graffiti, she says principals assigned each grade level a stairwell in which to paint a mural and restricted use of that stairwell to that grade level's students. The move, she says, has made them less likely to touch each other's work. She also simplified the uniforms for the lower school to khakis and white tops. Upper-school students get to add a maroon tie and blazer, plus each academy is now designing its own jacket patch. The upper-schoolers, she says, "feel a sense of pride" at getting to wear jackets and ties. Who would have imagined that formal dress would be perceived in an inner-city school as a reward?

Fix What's Not Working

Just because smart people have come up with a terrific research-based school design, it doesn't mean that it works in practice. Early studies on the New American School models focused on the quality of the models themselves, but more recently researchers looking at design success and failure have focused on implementation. How faithfully was the model executed?

In Hartford, Kishimoto recognized that during the 2008–2009 school year some new schools were struggling with this very issue. "We learned our lesson after year one," says Kishimoto, who says principals of the new schools were getting distracted by invitations to sit on district committees, by grant opportunities, by offers to partner to create new programs. "Every time someone came up to them and said, 'I have a great idea for a project or something I can do with these kids,' they thought every idea was a great idea. They didn't know how to say 'no' so they became overwhelmed."

The response was to change the supervisory model: instead of reporting to whichever head they would typically report to (say, assistant superintendent of secondary schools), new school principals now report to Kishimoto. They meet as a cohort on a monthly basis and are evaluated based on their fidelity to the models. "Before they can add a partner or explore a grant, I ask them what it helps them to do. I don't say 'yes' or 'no,' I say, 'Tell me how that aligns with your design.'" As a result, she sees a difference among the second cohort of principals whose schools opened in the 2009–2010 academic year. They are saying "no" to more invitations, plus they are more focused on teacher evaluations. Kishimoto says they have gotten her message: "You are not serving on any committees your first year; you are not leaving the building unless it is for professional development serving your design."

While new schools get three years to show improvement, Kishimoto says there is no sense waiting when a school is clearly headed off-track. At the Academy of Engineering and Green Technology, which opened in 2008–2009, she decided midway through the second year to remove the principal, Jacqueline Ryan, whom she described as a strong classroom teacher who was too weak in the sciences and wasn't getting it done as a leader. Because literacy is a problem across the district, Ryan had implemented "silent sustained reading" twice a week, on Mondays and Fridays, in *every* class, using twenty minutes for reading and ten minutes to answer writing prompts. That represented thirty minutes of each eighty-seven-minute class block. While Ryan felt she was addressing students' biggest deficit ("When you have students who are three to five years below grade level in reading, they can't access the content area as someone on grade level"), Kishimoto says for students drawn to hands-on programs in engineering and green technology that the approach was a mismatch. "You bore the kids to death."

There was a similar, though perhaps more dramatic, conflict at another second-year school, the Hartford Culinary Arts Academy, where Kishimoto says that classes designed to be project based were textbook focused. "You don't teach literacy by doing culinary themes," she says, noting that some teachers were trained as home economics teachers decades ago and had not updated their instruction styles to fit the new design. The school has also had the poorest test scores in the district. "Culinary implementation was so poor that they are now reporting to me," she says. She visited the building, dropped in on classroom lessons, and spoke with teachers. "It took my going into the classroom and saying, 'This is not *turn to page 43*.'"

However, the problems at the Culinary Arts Academy, located in a building with two other schools, went beyond pedagogy. "They were not controlling the culture. I would walk into the building and there would be kids hanging out in the hallways when they should be in class—and adults walking by them. There was nothing on the walls of classrooms. There were sports posters—this is a *culinary* school!—and trash in the hallways. I said, This is broken, it is so broken." Kishimoto concluded that "there were a lot of adult issues that were causing problems." She said, "They were just allowing the kids to wander all over the building. I started by telling the faculty they couldn't walk into the other school. I said, 'You may not visit another school unless you sign into the other school.'" She closed off some of the multiple entrances and exits to the building to separate the schools. She had a new sign made for the Culinary Arts Academy and gutted what was formerly the main office and converted it into a college and career center.

Midyear, in a move that angered the union, she hired a "director of culinary," a noncertified school position. For that post, Kishimoto brought in Debra Raviv, a woman who had run her own restaurant in Hartford and who had worked as a front-of-the-house and back-of-the-house trainer for the Max Restaurant Group, which has eight themed restaurants in Connecticut. "She knows how to work with a variety of young people who are not always well prepared to present themselves well," Kishimoto said, emphasizing that career-based academies like culinary need industry ties. By the spring of 2010, Raviv had placed twenty-five students in paid restaurant internships. Not surprisingly, the culinary school principal decided to resign at the end of the 2009–2010 school year, having come "to the conclusion that the school needed someone with more culinary expertise and more business entrepreneurship expertise," according to Kishimoto. She knows she will have to hire a new principal to oversee the traditional academic school operation but says that Raviv added a key ingredient: relevance to real-world work. "She has all these connections that a principal wouldn't necessarily have," says Kishimoto.

In addition, after recognizing that the old home economics facilities may have contributed to the school's identity problem, Kishimoto went through the budget and "moved money around" to come up with $1 million to build a state-of-the-art kitchen and restaurant. While it's unclear why this wasn't part of the original design and retrofitting process, her expectations going forward include more internships for students, opportunities for students to prepare food for community events, and creation of a student-run cooking show that can air on local television. Did Kishimoto's efforts pay off? It's too early to know for sure, but test scores released in July 2010 show that the percentage of culinary students meeting tenth-grade graduation requirements rose by 15.5 percent, the largest gain in the district.

"The biggest dilemma is how to find enough thought leaders," she says, "folks who understand where we are headed, the whole relevance piece of the curriculum, the rigor, and the relationship piece, faculty who understand they have to build a relationship with students, that this is not about standing and delivering a curriculum."

Unions Need to Be on the Team

To talk with Andrea Johnson, a sixth-grade teacher who herself graduated from Bulkeley High School (she won't say which year) and is president of the Hartford Federation of Teachers, is to hear about a parallel reality in Hartford schools. "They are good schools, good teachers, good kids," she says. "There are problems. Is there a major mess and nothing going on? Hardly, hardly."

She questions what education background Arne Duncan has that qualifies him to be secretary of education and lead a national reform effort. And Hartford superintendent Steven Adamowski, she says, has shown "that he doesn't have respect for this union." In this climate of radical reform, in which she says some administrators are "way out of the box," they are demanding teachers acclimate. Johnson feels there is too quick a trigger in wanting to toss out old teachers and hire in new.

"There is too much of 'Oh my god, you are not getting it, we need to get rid of you,'" says Johnson. "This whole reform is like, 'OK, let's get it done!' It is change. And change takes time."

Some of the tension Johnson expresses relates to the tone of the relationship between the district administration and union—and to the fact that Johnson feels they have not been included in discussions and formulations about reform. "It all comes down from the top guys, not from the folks who are doing the work. I am not too excited because we have not been part of the table seating," she says. "Where is the collaboration?"

Getting unions and school district leaders to be part of the same effort is one of the greatest challenges of the school turnaround movement. It is unclear how the differences will be resolved in Hartford, although conversations with some principals and teachers suggest that individual relationships within schools may be more functional than the head-butting at the district level. Still, one barrier is an old-style union stance that defends all teachers as a block, regardless of their performance, without differentiating or understanding breaks within the ranks. At the Ramon Betances Elementary School, which was closed at the end of the 2009–2010 school year, some teachers called in sick repeatedly, a behavior that frustrated other teachers who recognize that children—in this cases some of the poorest and neediest in the city—were still showing up to learn. "Every day when I come in and find out certain teachers are absent, I say to myself or a colleague, 'Do they work here or not?' It's really sad for the students, and it's hard on your colleagues when they have to take your students and they have to do two jobs," said Yvonne D'Eliseo, a third-grade teacher who had been at the school for eight years and spoke while the school was still open.

Teachers who are working hard and performing well don't want to be lumped with those who are slacking—and unions don't differentiate. This moment of dramatic reform represents a chance to recast teaching, to take it from a woe-is-me-overworked-underappreciated job to a movement of front-line professionals whose mission is every bit as valued as scientists' search for a cure for cancer. Adamowski, not surprisingly, believes teacher attitudes toward unions are shifting. Where education leaders who entered the profession in the 1960s saw union support as a social cause, he says that the same is not true for young people entering education today. "If you look at the Generation[s] X and Y, people who have five years of experience or less and most urban teachers from TFA [Teach for America], they are much more individually oriented. They seek efficacy for their work. They are not active in teachers unions. He says that "unions will have to change. They will have to play a different role."

Adamowski's suggestion—that there is a place for the union, but it may need to evolve—has been recognized elsewhere. American Federation of Teachers president Randi Weingarten, in a widely heralded speech at the National Press Club on January 12, 2010, said that traditional approaches needed a shake-up: "If we are going to thrive in the 21st century, our entire approach to education must change—from what goes on in the classroom, to how we care for children's well-being, to how labor and management work together." While she pushed back against the notion that troubled schools were the result of "bad teachers," arguing that "we face a systems problem," she did say that schools needed strong evaluation systems to develop high-quality teachers and get rid of ineffective ones. Such an admission, plus her call for a "fair and due-process system" (even though she has backed off this somewhat), leaves a lot of room for interpretation. But it is important because it recognizes that, as Adamowski suggests, unions must adapt to the needs of reform.

Already, some teacher unions are beginning to think more innovatively. In New Haven, a forty-five-minute drive down I-91 from Hartford, city officials and union leaders (with Weingarten's involvement) forged a new teacher contract that includes provisions for schoolwide performance pay based on student results. One of the most striking provisions is that schools labeled as "turnarounds" are to be reconstituted with new leadership and staff and are to be free from many union contract requirements (teachers who work in the turnaround school would have to commit for two years). While the contract does not address some other issues, it does raise concerns that the best teachers will just be plucked up by turnaround principals with the less effective ones reshuffled into other schools. But progress is dramatic enough that Dacia Toll of Achievement First says they have discussed partnering with Scott Given, CEO and co-founder of UP (Unlocking Potential) Schools, to turnaround an existing New Haven city school in the future. Toll says the freedom to hire teachers, including existing New Haven union teachers, while having flexibility about expectations and work conditions is what makes this attractive. "Basically, it allows an operator to come in and assign the terms of work," she says. Teachers "have to be union members, but we don't have to take the existing union contract."

There are signs of union flexibility elsewhere, too, and some has come not from broad union concession but from school leaders taking a different stance. Furman Brown, cofounder of Generation Schools, a New York City district school that employs charter-style innovative uses of time says that when he and cofounder Jonathan Spear sought to open their high school as one of several smaller schools in the former South Shore High School building in Brooklyn, they made clear that they wanted to work *with* the teacher union.

Brown, who in the early 1990s taught fifth grade in South Central Los Angeles as part of Teach for America, says, "We didn't look at them as the enemy. We said, 'All right, let's try to anticipate what they would think it would take for a great teacher to thrive, what are the things that make the job really difficult?"

When conversations with both New York City school department and union leaders began, with Furman and Spear trying to put themselves in teachers' shoes, they developed workplace models that were practical in nature (albeit using an out-of-the-box school calendar and school design). They respected time for teacher planning and rejuvenation; teachers get large chunks of time off from teaching duties during the academic year. So while the design is unorthodox, the union embraced it. "We didn't try to create a model that was union-friendly," says Brown, "but we learned that workplace success is a shared goal of everybody."

And while Brown was at first frustrated by a union demand for a twenty-minute break between two long morning academic classes (what they call "foundation courses"), he and Spear gave in. "It turned out to be a great use of time," says Brown, who says the break has become a time to meet with a teacher, have a snack, and take a breather before refocusing. "I just had a snack before our phone call," he quipped.

Teaching Parents to Expect More

One of the big questions about inner-city education reform is whether parents—and not the block of "education choosers," but average parents—will become invested enough to be a force in reform. Particularly in a portfolio district like Hartford, parental input matters. If families decide a school is ineffective and don't enroll their children, that should, in theory, spur on change and improvement.

In Hartford, families with children enrolling for the first time, enrolling in kindergarten or ninth grade, or returning to the district after being away for a year are required to select a school (one can transfer any time, though preference in placement goes to those required to choose). Families must submit their choices online by the end of March, and students are notified of their placement by mid-April. (Despite initial concerns that many parents would not fill out choice applications online only in spring 2010, Kishimoto says applications increased from spring 2009, when parents could fill out applications on paper or online. She says there were several registration sessions at the public library in which parents with various linguistic backgrounds were trained to help other parents register. At one session, Kishimto reports "the line was out the door.") Parents then have until the end of April to accept or decline the district's placement for their child. This choice opportunity—amplified by the district's child-based budgeting—means parent education matters.

In 2009 ConnCAN and Trinity College launched a Web site to help parents navigate their options. The district also holds several city-wide school choice fairs, where families can gather information and ask questions of principals. One was held on a mid-December Saturday at Hartford Public High School. In a sign of interest, the parking lot was full. People pulled alongside fences and squeezed at odd angles near the service areas at the rear of the building. Parents with children and ex-tended families weaved through vehicles to reach the front doors. And this was a full half hour before the official 9 A.M. start!

Inside the school's cavernous athletic complex, principals, like mer-chants at a bazaar, stood beside displays and tried to lure passersby into conversations—sales' pitches, really—about their schools. They pressed glossy brochures into any willing hand. There were banners, balloons, candy, a live drummer, and the Bulkeley High School bull-dog mascot.

"The principals actually have to market their school," says Kishim-oto, who during the fair took a break from checking in with princi-pals to have a conversation in an available quiet space, in this case the girls' locker room. Sitting beside a rack of basketballs, she said she ap-preciated many of the efforts but said some principals still don't fully appreciate the stakes. "In the past you would have your clientele," she observed. "Now parents can vote with their feet. Essentially you can have a school that doesn't have families applying and enrollment goes down. If enrollment goes down, then we would have a conversation about the viability of the school."

This is the second year of choice fairs, and families are learning, too. "Last year they were more nervous about going in and asking a prin-cipal or staff member about their school," says Kishimoto. "Last year, they were just repeating basic information from the flyers, 'So your school hours are . . . ?'" Now, she observes, there are conversations about afterschool programming, how teachers are hired, and even spe-cific design elements of the school. "Those are great quality questions," she says.

The power structure has tipped—or, more accurately, is tipping. Parents at the fair may not think about Adamowski's performance matrix or where a particular school falls on it, but they do sense change.

Juanna Campos, a 1997 Bulkeley High graduate who works as a warehouse temp "packing things into boxes," has come with her sister's family; her niece needed to choose a high school. She is also here with her own two daughters, a fourth grader with stylish purple-framed glasses and a kindergartner who says she wants to be a model. Campos is proud that her older daughter earns As and Bs, loves math, and might want to become a doctor. She also hopes that all this reform is for real and means that her daughter really will have options she didn't have. "I went to high school, but I didn't have these choices," she says. "I want her to be something big."

The turnaround mood is apparent to another city school alum at the fair. Gabriel Rosario, a military police dog handler and 1993 graduate of A.I. Prince Technical High School, came of age in the Hartford of gangs and teachers who "were afraid to teach." "This is like 180-degrees different from when I was growing up," he says, as he meanders with his wife, Yesenia, and their two daughters, ages two and twelve, pausing at any school with a performance arts–related program (his eldest's passion). He may not be ready to sift through all the available information coming his way, but Rosario is moved not just by the school choices for his children but by what it could mean for Hartford. "You know, I am really proud of this city for being this kind of a system," he says. "If you can do this and mold our kids, imagine what it will be like here twenty years from now?"

3

SCHOOL-LEVEL LESSONS

B ACK IN 2001, ANTHONY G. SMITH—neighborhood kid made good from Cincinnati's West End—was handed a job that many people didn't want. And to be fair, he wasn't sure he wanted it either. In fact, it was after Smith, a successful middle school principal in the city, made one more visit to Taft High School after Superintendent Steven Adamowski had offered him the principal's post that he decided the place was just too troubled for him to fix. Smith got in his car and headed downtown to let Adamowski know that he wasn't the guy. But when Smith arrived, Adamowski—with reporters and TV cameras nearby, as Smith recalls—didn't let him speak. "He walked me into the room and said, 'Here's Anthony Smith. He's the new principal at Taft High School, and he's going to say a few words.'"

There was good reason for Smith to be hesitant. Every academic indicator suggested problems, and the school culture was chaotic, dangerous, and unproductive. A 1999 case study of the school by several Taft teachers and University of Miami researchers described a "dark and impersonal building." In a symbol of the malaise, they noted a swimming pool out of use for five years because it was in disrepair. And signs posted at building entrances practically begged parents to care: "Proficiency Tests March 2–13. Must pass to graduate. Talk to your child" and "200 students absent or tardy daily! Is this your child? Come in and see."

Turnaround, Then and Now

A lot has changed since 2001—both for Taft and in terms of public interest in the failings of high-poverty urban schools. At the time Smith took over, turnaround as a neat public policy concept didn't exist the way it does today. Yet, the experience of Smith's transformation of this school, and his commonsense approach to driving change by building relationships, might as well be lesson one in the school turnaround text (if such a thing existed). Yes, leaders matter, but it's what those leaders do to rally talent, support, and help (from inside and out) that is bedrock in turnaround.

At the time Smith took over, well below 30 percent of students who entered in ninth grade made it to graduation. He also encountered things that just didn't make sense: the start time for a teacher's day, 8 A.M., was the same for students. Lunch period was so disorganized that it lasted for nearly two hours a day and left kids eating in the hallways. The school was not a respite from but, rather, recycled the culture of shootings and violence that existed in the neighborhood. And far from evincing pride, the school's sports teams barely existed. Players would quit, making it impossible for teams to finish the season.

And yet today Taft High School, renamed Robert A. Taft Information Technology High School, was selected as a 2010 Blue Ribbon School and named a School of Promise by the Ohio Department of Education. In 2008–2009, 98 percent of students scored "proficient" or "advanced" on both state reading and math tests required for graduation. The school has moved from being in "academic emergency," the lowest state school designation, to being "effective," the second highest, meeting eleven out of twelve state indicators. In 2010, it was named "excellent," Ohio's highest rating. They have a full complement of sports teams and even lured former Cincinnati Bengals wide receiver Mike Martin to revive the football program.

One characteristic of school-level turnaround today is that the timetable has been collapsed. Results are expected to come quickly—though it remains a matter of debate *how quickly* it is possible to go from poor to terrific. Despite some key early support, a better school atmosphere, and kids even working harder, it took time for Taft test scores to rise, says Michael Turner, a key Taft administrator who oversees the technology program. "Because you have dramatic culture change does not mean you have a data change," he says, noting that the school for a few years after Smith arrived remained in academic emergency, that bottom designation.

The challenge, observes Turner, is that when school performance is so low to begin with, it cannot be instantly raised. "When you've got a school with a 12 to 18 percent graduation rate, a 30 percent dropout rate, a 60 percent attendance rate, I don't know how it's humanly possible to turn around a school like that in one year or two. It took us three to four years before we saw some major changes." In fact, state test data show that as recently as the 2004–2005 academic year, just 40 percent of Taft students scored "proficient" or higher in math and 64 percent in reading. But data also show a dramatic leap the next year (2005–2006), perhaps reflecting the first cohort of students to go through the transformed high school from start to finish. For those students, 88 percent scored "proficient" or higher in math and 91 percent in reading, scores that have continued to rise.

"My covenant is with the community"

What's notable about Taft's turnaround—and Smith will tell you it is still being "turned around" (they are scheduled to move into a brand new school building in December 2010)—is that it has happened without starting fresh or importing a new teaching staff. Taft has been transformed with the same teachers and the same students. But it is certainly not the same school.

At the heart of what Smith has done is repair and build relationships—relationships between the school and the community, between the school and business leaders, and between and among teachers and students. "I don't think the superintendent asked me to come to Taft by coincidence," Smith says today. For his part, Adamowski says he saw in Smith "a missionary zeal to do things that had not been done before to raise student achievement." And, like a missionary, Smith first brought his message about school turnaround to the community around Taft, asking for residents' consideration and support to make the school someplace they would send their kids.

After all, when he took over, Smith, himself a 1973 Taft grad, was crushed to see that the West End neighborhood of predominantly poor African Americans and a few Appalachian whites had turned its back on the school. Parents were sending their teens elsewhere in the city if they could. For this neighborhood, where 53 percent of households live below the poverty line (the median household income is $12,219) and only 55 percent of adults have a high school diploma, that was a serious dis. So one of the first things Smith did was go out and, door to door, court the people of the West End. He told them he needed their help to turn the school around.

"My covenant was with the community, not necessarily with the board of education," Smith says, reflecting an understanding that while schools are part of districts, they are also part of the community and people's lives. "The people in the neighborhood were my people. I knew the parents of the kids, the grandparents of the kids, the aunts, the uncles. We asked them to support us, to send their kids, support us in athletics, come to activities, some to senior night, come to parent night."

A Handshake, a Paint Job, Cell Phones, and Laptops

When he started, Smith made a few important moves that turned out to be essential to the school's successful trajectory, including forming a key relationship with Cincinnati Bell. Smith and Jack Cassidy, CEO of Cincinnati Bell, met when they ended up sitting next to one another at a school board meeting. Cassidy says he came to the meeting at the request of his friend, Steve Adamowski. When Cassidy sat down beside Smith and asked him what he did, he could not believe that such a polished and well-dressed gentleman was the principal of what was considered the worst high school in the city. "I can tell right now by looking at you that you're not!" Cassidy recalls exclaiming. Smith deadpanned, "I just got the job."

Before the meeting ended, the two shook hands and agreed to find a way to work together. Soon after, Cassidy made a trip to the school. When he pulled up in a company-owned black Suburban, he claims, "I saw a bunch of kids running to flush drugs down the toilet because they were sure the DEA was there." Cassidy says that after visiting he was appalled that taxpayer money was funding such failure. He wanted to be involved. "We met with Anthony and his staff and tried to understand where it was they wanted to go and how we might help."

The relationship Smith and Cassidy built is today touted as a model for school-corporate relations. Volunteers from Cincinnati Bell tutor students to help them pass state tests, and the company offers Taft students paid internships, college scholarships, and—something that gave a kick to student academic focus—a free phone and use of a laptop for technology program students who maintain a 3.3 GPA. When the cell phone and laptop incentives began, observed tenth-grade biology teacher Cheryle Kelleher, she saw student effort change for the better. "That was the first time I remember students being concerned about their grades. It was that dramatic a change," she says. "Suddenly, students were coming to me and asking, 'Why did I get a C?' How can I get a B?' I didn't think they cared."

As part of the partnership with Cincinnati Bell, in a gesture that teachers vividly recall as an important moment, on June 9, 2001, before the "new" school opened as the Taft Information Technology High School, 600 company employees and community volunteers arrived at the school. Within hours they had repainted hallways and lockers in vibrant colors and landscaped around the building. They even repaired and painted an announcer's booth on the football field. A year later, on June 15, 2002, 225 volunteers painted classrooms and, from money the company raised from community partners, replaced all the blinds in the school. The fact that the painting effort came from volunteers, including Bell employees who lived in the community, some of whom had attended Taft themselves, says Smith, created a connection and pride that had the added bonus of minimizing graffiti.

Change, with the Same Teachers

Another key move Smith made was counterintuitive: he kept the staff he inherited at Taft. When he took the job, Smith did bring a few people with him from his previous school, including Michael Turner, whose title is senior institute manager and program facilitator but who is better known as Smith's right-hand man. He also brought a team of four middle school teachers (including Cheryle Kelleher), letting them stay together and loop with incoming students through tenth grade. Not only were they his people who understood his expectations, but Smith felt that they could aid transition to high school for new ninth graders.

But Smith's decision not to fire the staff and start fresh runs counter to conventional wisdom about how to fix troubled schools. Old teachers, the thinking goes, resist change and prevent transformation. And yet, Smith insists, "we reinvented our culture by building healthy relationships." In August 2001, as teachers were preparing classrooms for the start of the school year, Smith dropped by their rooms and interviewed each teacher individually for an hour. "I asked them what was good, what was bad, and how they were willing to change to make the place better. It gave me a sense of whether they wanted to be here. People can say different things in groups, but I wanted to hear from them individually. At the end of the day, I realized that despite my preconceived notions, that they really did want the school to get better."

The sense that there were good teachers caught in a broken school also struck Smith after his first staff meeting one August morning. He made it plain that there was a lot of work to do, and that at this moment they were failing, given the school's official academic emergency status. "I said, 'We are at the bottom of the totem pole. This is the worst you can be.' I asked them, 'How do you feel about possibly being the worst school in the entire state?'" Before they took a break, Smith laid it out: "If you don't think you can do it the way we need to do it for students to succeed, don't come back after lunch." To his surprise, they all returned. "I believe they were good teachers. They had lost their confidence. They had lost their spirit."

One of those teachers, Jocelynne Jason, says it was apparent from her first meeting with Smith that he was a different kind of leader who expects a lot but who also motivates teachers to perform. "He plopped down in a chair and chatted with me. He came to the quick realization that I knew what I was doing." Jason does not claim that Smith "is like Merlin the magician," but after their first meeting she told Michael Turner that "he makes me want to be a better teacher."

Smith's relationship with teachers, however, does carry some tension. Results of a 2009 Cincinnati Public Schools teacher survey conducted by the district suggest that some consider him too authoritative. On a series of questions about administrative attention to teacher opinions, teachers at Taft rated Smith lower than district peers rated their principals on the support they received. He can be tough, says Jason. "I'm not happy with him a good portion of the time—he drives me nuts! There are times I think he is a dictator," she says. "But how can you deny the success he has had?"

In Turnaround: Law and Government Academy

Sometimes the stuff you are not supposed to notice captures the essence of a school's challenge. In this case, several boys in the hallway of the Law and Government Academy on a December morning are dressed in the school's required uniform: white dress shirt, striped tie, blazer (or LGA logo sweater) slacks, and dress shoes. But while they technically meet the letter of the dress code, they wear their pants so low (and ties so askew) as to evoke a look that is more high-style hip-hop than aspiring law clerk. It's an odd sight, but a reminder that although adults are willing students into professional futures, the kids themselves are still teenagers living in the moment. The tension is central to turnaround schools like this one: How can you get students to see far enough ahead to realize the value—the need, really—to work hard now?

Unlike Taft, which is now tweaking programming and building on what leaders know works, the Law and Government Academy is urgently searching for a set of approaches that will yield results. One of four smaller schools formed in 2008 in the quest to turnaround Hartford Public High School, Law and Government Academy adopted a dress code as a tool designed to alert students to new expectations. The gap between dress code image and living reality, between fresh expectations and old failure, however, is not lost on Adam Johnson, the school's Harvard-educated, ginger-ale-drinking principal. "These kids are growing up in neighborhoods where people are perpetually unemployed, and we are preparing them for careers that require postgraduate education," he says, suggesting that his job is not purely to get students to achieve academically but to acquire the polish and bearings to pursue middle-class lives. "I need to get them to see what Hartford looks like from the twenty-sixth floor. I need them to see that it is within their grasp to attain."

It may be a leap for students, most of whom receive free or reduced-price lunches, to imagine themselves in professions earning high five- or six-figure incomes. But that is what Johnson sees as the underlying purpose of this turnaround mission: lighting a fire. In fact, that idea is so central to his vision that when staff and students were debating the design of a school logo, Johnson nixed images of gavels and scales of justice to settle on a bright-red flame. "We are not just about courts and justice. We need to be about more than that," he says, noting that the flame suggests passion. "When we defined our driving forces, passion was primary—that students would be passionate in their courses, passionate in the work that they were doing."

It is, however, one thing to hold lofty dream of engaged students enraptured by their work—Johnson envisions students one day running campaigns to shepherd laws through the state legislature or holding mock press conferences and historical debates about whether to start the Civil War—and another to actually scale the mountain before him. In September, for example, formative assessments showed that 57 percent of entering tenth graders scored at the "below basic" level in reading and another 9 percent scored in the "basic" category. That means that in September—the September of the year that students take the Connecticut Academic Performance Test (CAPT) required for graduation—two-thirds were below grade level in reading, with the majority of those *several* grade levels below. When Johnson describes students in "below basic," he says that they cannot read fluently and understand the material.

This represents a stunning challenge. The job of getting students "proficient" is made tougher because, since it's a grade 10–12 school, teachers do not have these students as ninth graders but must prepare them in just a few months for the CAPT test. Plus, because Connecticut has no statewide ninth-grade test (students in grades 3–8 take the Connecticut Mastery Test, or CMT), Johnson reads his students' old eighth-grade test scores as academic tea leaves. How much growth did they make in ninth grade? Unknown. And this is not to forget that the school, and Johnson himself, are judged on whether they are dramatically raising student scores.

Given the "no excuses" phrase that has become cliché in urban school reform, Johnson can't really complain. His job is to *do*, which is why small successes are tempered by a persistent uncertainty. Johnson says there have been times when he "definitely worried" that he might be fired or replaced. "Had that type of conversation happened, it wouldn't have shocked me," he says, although he mentions recently receiving positive feedback. "There are other schools where the principals have been removed, and I'm not one of them. The fact that right now I am safe is a pretty important thing to me."

The need to show results—and quickly—feeds an obvious tension. Johnson wants to reach out and help struggling urban kids discover their inner student, but he needs kids motivated and able to work hard. Plus, in a system in which money follows the student, he wants his school to be a top choice—but for the right students. Too many kids who sign on and slack off could put him out of business. This pressure is very real to Johnson but must surely be an unintended consequence of turnaround policy, which probably doesn't want principals of nonmagnets prowling for the best students and finding ways to dissuade or nudge out those who can't cut it. And yet Johnson is not the only principal to describe this tension. Other turnaround school leaders and and even district schools facing competition from charters are quick to make the accusation that charters might accept any student but that not all of them can do what's expected, and that every year some students leave charters and return to district schools. The consequence is an underclass of the underclass in education. Who will educate those students? Who will be responsible for helping them achieve academically and pass state tests?

At the same time, this aspect of school turnaround contributes to a certain amount of marketing, healthy competition, and an effort by principals to create the right buzz around their school. There is, in other words, a drive to be a recognized winner that will attract the best students. This was in evidence during the December citywide school choice fair. On that Saturday morning, as Johnson fiddled with a display, he wasn't exactly nervous, but he was aware of the stakes. He reminded two staffers of the goal when talking with families: "If they say, 'Oh, I'm thinking of going to a magnet school, we should say, 'Check this out,'" offering a brochure in a practice gesture. His goal, of course, is to compete for students who would otherwise be drawn to the city's best-performing schools with high percentages of students passing the state tests. At the same time, he admits to discouraging slackers. "I tell freshmen, 'If you don't like doing homework, don't come to Law and Government Academy,'" and then he throws in mention of the demanding dress code. "I say, 'If you don't like wearing ties, don't come to Law and Government Academy.'"

From Paper Plan to Real School

Before Adam Johnson was even hired to be principal, the Law and Government Academy had a plan. On December 18, 2007, the design team led by Bridget Allison, a Georgetown University law school grad and

Washington, D.C., civil litigation lawyer–turned teacher, presented the plan to the Hartford Board of Education. The design described the theme—law, government, community leadership—along with details about the mission, the governance structure, length of school day (7:40 a.m. to 3:25 p.m.), and even what activities students should engage in (moot court, mock trial) and what courses should be offered. The document contains exuberant, reform-friendly language, like rigor, exceeding standards for academic and social success, continuous collaboration, and learning partnership.

Despite a plan with good vibes and lots of detail, Johnson says the most challenging issue they wrangled with in Year One was their identity off the paper: "We needed to figure out who we are and what we are trying to do." Interpretation, in other words, is huge. That piece of work began when Johnson and Allison, now dean of students at the school, went about hiring a staff. Johnson says they received 400 applications for twenty-three openings. Although he was hiring for the new school while the old Hartford Public High School was still operating, he worked through the question, Who do you rehire? Christina Kishimoto, Hartford assistant superintendent for school design, says their district's redesign approach favors a large staff turnover. She says that "to have a real change process, you want a 50 to 70 percent change."

Johnson purposely made the application process tough, sending e-mails to applicants with questions about niggling details in their letters of recommendation. His rationale: "I want you to see that I have my game together and if you are not ready to bring it, this is not the school for you," he says. "I tried to scare them away." Johnson wanted individuals who could manage both the pressure and challenge of a turnaround, of doing the nearly impossible job of taking kids reading at elementary and middle school grade levels and preparing them for college—in three years.

He spent time observing teachers in the Hartford Public High School building, and his judgments, while harsh, reflect the need to hire people who would be quick off the mark and would be compelled by the serious learning gaps. "I was asking myself, 'Has this person been able to become a good teacher—or even an adequate teacher—in a corrupt school? Has this person been able to teach, love working with kids in a toxic environment—or are they too far gone?" An added tension for Johnson was that Allison was both his design team chair and a teacher at the old school who had friends in the building. He worried she would lobby to hire them.

Nonetheless, they worked together from the start, and Allison, who was deeply invested in the planning, wasn't about to hire people into *her* school who she didn't think were excellent. As she looked at colleagues, she admits, "there were a number of teachers, some were burned out and some weren't good to begin with." At that time, they were able to hire teachers from outside the district (tougher to do now), which Allison says was "crucially important. If you are going to create a themed school and you are trying to change things around, you need people who are on board—and you want to be picky about that. You don't want to be forced to take someone because they are on a list. You want to take the best." In the end, they only rehired eight teachers.

The work of the first year, says Johnson, in addition to being about the identity of the school, focused on their identity as a *professional culture*. "It was about, 'How do we work together?'" he says. In any school, and in turnaround schools in particular, teacher collaboration is fundamental to the mission. There is so much ground to make up, so many holes to identify and address, that teachers simply *must* work together as a team. Most likely, a problem in English is also a problem in history, particularly in a district like Hartford that has a root weakness in reading. As a result, Johnson created teams of teachers both by grade level and also by subject area. He formalized and standardized expectations (in writing) for how those teams would operate and what collaborative work would look like.

He followed that up by having several staff members attend a conference on using data so that could become a focus of teamwork the second year. He says it has taken work to get past data anxieties to get at *what* about the data matters. "Data does not mean complex equations or *r squared*," he says. "Once we simplified things, it helped get people on the same page." For example, he says, English teachers in their work together "talk a lot about questions three and four" of the CAPT. Those are open-ended questions, with question three testing how students make connections to literature and question four challenging students to take a critical stance and evaluate what an author is trying to do. This has fed team brainstorming and problem-solving sessions. Says Johnson, "My English department spent a lot of collaborative time asking themselves, 'How are they doing here?' and 'How can we teach them better?'"

Is It Working?

In March of Year Two, Johnson believes that his students still aren't working hard enough. While he doesn't know yet how they performed on the CAPT tests, he hopes that some positive signs he sees will translate into results. By January, students had taken three rounds of formative assessments to predict their scores, and data showed improvement. The percentage of tenth graders in "below basic" and "basic"—likely to fail the state test—has dropped from two-thirds to 49 percent of students. In writing, 38 percent of students are now poised to pass, up from just 21 percent in September. And in math, the percentage likely to pass rises from 11 to 23 percent. Still dismal, but it is progress.

In a stab to boost scores even more by test time, on December 3 Johnson sent out an invitation to twenty-five of the lowest-performing students. "Congratulations!" the letter reads, "You are one of a small group of Law & Government Academy 10th graders invited to attend a special program to help you improve your performance on the CAPT." Besides reminding students that passing CAPT is required for graduation, he offers an enticement to lure them to prep sessions on eight Saturday mornings: perfect attendance earns them an 8GB iPod Touch, "a $199 value!" He asks interested invitees to "please write a short, handwritten note to Mr. Johnson expressing your intention." Nineteen students signed up and attended.

While Johnson appears to be making strides, it's fair to ask, Is it enough? In 2007, after all, Hartford Public High School had 36.9 percent of students reach "proficient" or higher in reading, 36.7 percent in writing, and 30 percent in math. Is the Law and Government Academy doing anything scorewise that the old troubled high school wasn't?

Allison says the school today has a different and dramatically better climate. The old school, she says, was a "Darwinian survival of the fittest. There was no kind of support; there was no curriculum." But she worries about showing that shift in test data. "We've had some successes, but those successes have not been measurable," she says. "I sometimes have serious doubts about whether we will be able to get the numbers they want us to get given the students we have coming up, kids who are on the third- and fourth-grade reading levels in tenth grade."

What do the numbers, such as they are, show? When 2009–2010 test results are released, Johnson is pleased. At 7:28 p.m. on July 14, 2010, he sends an e-mail message whose subject line reads, "Scores are in," and the body of the message says simply, "and they are good!" Results show a 21 percent increase in the percentage of students scoring proficient or higher in reading (now 53 percent) and a 10–65 percent rise in writing. The results are less good in math (down 4 percent to 31 percent) and essentially unchanged in science, in which only about one-fourth of students met the standard. Still, for a school focused on reading and writing skill areas, this represents progress. The nagging question, however, is, Is it enough? Math scores, for example, don't seem to be a lot better than what the old Hartford Public High School managed to produce. And certainly, it's hard to celebrate when large percentages of students are still failing.

What the analysis is missing, though, is important: the old high school test scores, like graduation test score data at schools across the country, reflect a *cumulative* score of all those who have passed the test in grades 10, 11, and 12, whereas the Law and Government Academy data is reflecting the scores of first-time tenth-grade test-takers. It's an unfortunate reality that some students spend much of their high school careers trying to meet the tenth-grade standard.

At the end of Year Two, the finish line—is still far off, but Johnson feels more settled and confident than he did earlier in the school year. On a damp, late-March evening, after leaving a meeting of the school governance council, which is composed of parents, a student, several staff members, an outside coach, the school's family liaison, and Johnson, he is ebullient. Only schools that are doing well—in the "autonomous" or "defined autonomy" categories—get to have a school governance council (poorly performing schools have lots of district intervention instead). "I got one and I love it!" he says. "I see it as being very crucial for laying the groundwork for the future. We are a young school and we are a developing school. We have a vision, but we are still figuring things out."

One council task was preparing the budget, which meant working through a key decision to hire a second school counselor instead of another English teacher. There were debates about whether an English teacher was more critical, given how far behind so many kids are in reading and writing. But, says Johnson, the school does have three English teachers, a reading teacher, two English as a second language (ESL) teachers, and several reading tutors. And there is only a single counselor, who Johnson says "is very good, but she's swamped." She is so overwhelmed that many sophomores have no clue about the things they must do to make college attainable, from getting involved in extracurricular activities to preparing for the SATs to getting their grades up. "You don't change a kid's mind and get them to develop the proper mentality in the fall of their junior year," says Johnson. "Quite frankly, a kid may have burned too many bridges for themselves by then."

What was important about the council's decision and the debate that got them to it, he says, was that they hashed over matters central to the school's focus and identity. The discussion was an exercise in expressed vision, in hope, in concrete plans. "How you operationalize a budget is such a reflection of the school's mission," he says. "When we looked at our guidance program, it was retrograde. In our mission statement is 'college.' Kids are here to go to college."

Seeking New Approaches: Role for Charters?

Johnson feels the pressure of making up for lost time in his students' academic careers. And while the sprint to get kids many years behind up to grade level and ready to do college-level work at times sounds ridiculously ambitious, this is the very point of turnaround. This spotlight moment in education, after all, calls for tearing up old plans and finding new and better ways to do the work of educating these students. One way to do this is to find leaders and programs that have already thought about this challenge and found some success. That is why U.S. education secretary Arne Duncan has asked the nation's high-performing charter schools and education management organizations to come into cities and take over failing schools. A few organizations have stepped up, including Green Dot in Los Angeles and Mastery in Philadelphia. Most top charter organizations, however, have preferred to start schools fresh rather than untangle an existing mess. It's worth understanding why so many are reticent to play a role in district school turnaround.

One of the most obvious candidates to engage in district turnaround would seem to be KIPP, the Knowledge Is Power Program, which has a network of eighty-two charter schools in nineteen states and the District of Columbia, with plans to grow to 100 by the 2011–2012 school year. But the program is, for now, staying away from the restart model (how Duncan describes taking over existing district schools) despite reported urgings directly from the U.S. Department of Education. "We've had a lot of conversations with Duncan's office and he understands," says Steve Mancini, director of public affairs for KIPP. "Clearly, we have a sense of urgency, but we also have a sense of what our limitations are, what we can do."

When Mancini speaks of the organization's limitations, he is referring to a failed foray into district turnaround in Denver. The reasons for this failed effort may or may not be relevant to other charter organizations and districts. But their experience does highlight cultural and structural differences that must be well thought out in order for collaboration to take place. The message is this: although charters and districts may be doing the same sort of work—educating students—the differences in their approaches must be acknowledged and accounted for. In 2005 KIPP entered a competition and was selected to take over the bottom-performing Cole Middle School. Not KIPP's usual approach, the plan called for the school to be only grades 7 and 8 the first year with existing students; the second year it would become eighth grade only, while KIPP would also start a new fifth grade, which was more aligned with their grades 5–8 approach.

But at the end of the second year, KIPP pulled out. While students made some academic progress, Mancini says the arrangement was fraught with problems. The governance structure saddled the school with essentially two boards—one local and one national—and, he says, "too many players." They also failed to attract the top-level leader they wanted (plus they did not have time for the usual full year of training). The school ended up with three principals in the first three months of operation and never found the right leader to start the fifth-grade program. In addition, Mancini says, the school had become such a symbol of the achievement gap in the city that no one wanted to step into such a supercharged setting. "It was a powder keg locally. Every [potential] leader knew there was a lot of scrutiny. People knew, 'If I take this job, on Day One I will have a TV truck outside my school,'" he says. "The Denver experience was very sobering for us."

Mancini's point, together with the KIPP experience, suggests an important lesson in turnaround: baggage can be trouble, and sometimes having new people at the top—even with new ideas—is not enough. Like restaurants that fail in the same cursed location, schools marked as troubled can have a difficult time shaking the identity and culture of failure. Tinkering around the edges won't get it done.

This also raises questions about *how* districts should work with charter organizations. According to Dacia Toll, whose Achievement First has a school within the Hartford District and which may in the future consider partnering to turn around a New Haven city school, creating clear lines of authority matters. Charters want control over aspects of school governance, hiring, and work rules that districts may not be used to, or comfortable, offering. The challenge for both districts and charters is to find the philosophical common ground that can make the structural details negotiable. It must be—and is—possible to combine serious innovation and district (and union) cultures. Brooklyn Generation Academy is a New York City district school, not a charter, that has NYC union teachers *and,* at the same time, has profoundly rearranged the school calendar to help students play academic catch-up while giving them exposure to careers and concrete job skills. In other words, it thinks and acts like a charter school but is mindful of the district school's contract-based pressures.

Brooklyn Generation: Use Time Differently

When Furman Brown sought to help turn around a failing Brooklyn, New York, high school in the borough's Canarsie section, he was clear that basic things in inner-city schools were not working. Success, he insisted, could not happen by changing just one piece. "We can't just reform; we need to reinvent," says Brown, who, before approaching the takeover, spent ten years thinking about the challenges of inner-city high schools. He describes working through what he calls "the Rubik's Cube that is a school" by taking everything out of the garage and putting it back in a different way.

The most striking concept to emerge forms the basis for the Brooklyn Generation School: a fundamentally fresh use of time. The school has a calendar that gives students a 200-day school year without adding teacher time. The schedule recasts the school year in blocks that stagger teacher vacations and twice a year give teachers four weeks off (three weeks to rest and one to plan). While some teachers get a break, other teachers lead students in month-long project-based "intensives" that, for example, in ninth grade include private-sector hands-on experiences in fields such as health, technology, law, and banking; in tenth grade expand to have students adopt a cause like Doctors Without Borders and do real-life work to effect change; and by eleventh grade have them participate in internships and college programs. Seniors are scheduled for an intensive guidance program to work on college applications, essays, and financial aid and to do "life-readiness" training. "This is independent work and group work, it is project-based work driven by deadlines and goals," says Brown, adding that while such skills are critical to life success, many schools don't teach them. "Part of our whole college and career program is connecting learning to life. We are trying to help kids understand the value of getting really good at something."

The Generation Schools model also uses time differently during the school day. Each morning students have two ninety-minute "foundation" classes that include a math/science block and a humanities block covering the subjects that are on the state Board of Regents exams. These classes have just fourteen to sixteen students, giving teachers time to work individually and in small groups. While the courses address state exam subjects, Brown is adamant that the point is not passing tests but teaching students to think deeply about issues. "If the only reason we are studying world history is to pass the dang test, let's just whip through it," he says. "But that is not the only reason. To solve the challenges in the world, it helps to have people develop skills in debating and negotiating and problem solving and communicating opinions in different ways."

In the afternoon, students take three-hour-long "studio" courses (with class sizes of twenty-four to twenty-eight) that are leveled according to student needs (Brown says 80 percent of students are behind or far behind grade level, but some are ready for an honors sequence). For example, some students may take courses in algebra II, finance, accounting, engineering, robotics, foreign language, filmmaking, or digital media while others get credit recovery, test prep, or special education help.

Two things are key in the Brooklyn Generation approach. First, the model places an emphasis on the personalization of learning according to student needs and interests, which optimizes student learning time, something critical for kids who are behind. Second, the model recognizes that teachers have different strengths and preferences. Most teachers are dual-role teachers who teach two foundation courses and one studio course each day; others are single-role teachers who focus on a single subject (perhaps teaching studio courses) and then may serve in nonteaching school positions; and there are also "intensive" teachers who lead the month-long project-based courses and rotate twice a year to each grade. This differentiation allows a flexibility that is uncommon in teaching. "It's not that we have more people," says Brown, "we just use them differently." But the most impressive part of the model is that all of it—even providing teachers with two hours per day of planning time—works within existing budgets and with NYC public school teachers under the existing union contract.

The school is a district school, founded as a partnership between the city's department of education, the United Federation of Teachers, and Generation Schools. To get everyone on board, says Brown, he and Spear began by connecting the dots: a better environment for teachers is a better environment for student learning and better student learning is a win for everyone. "Two things we heard all the time is, 'You can't change the system' and 'You can't work with the unions,'" Brown says. "We said, 'You *have* to change the system' and 'You *have* to work with the unions.'" After getting the teacher union and the school district to agree to the model, the Brooklyn Generation School opened in the fall of 2007 with ninth graders. The first year they received 201 applications for eighty-one seats. (Each year they have added a grade; the first class will graduate in 2011.)

New Start in a Troubled School

While the Brooklyn Generation School is based on fresh thinking, it has opened in what parents and students have known for years was a low-performing, even dangerous, public school building. South Shore High School, with its dismal 36 percent graduation rate and 67 percent daily student attendance, has been a fixture of failure. When it was built in 1969, the hulking 404,000-square-foot, 170-classroom structure may have been a salute to modernism; today it looks like an outdated cross between a federal prison and the Starship Enterprise. With its four-story-high white brick-and-stone facade (with a curved front and two Enterprise-like arms connecting big "boxes" [gym and auditorium] on each side) and diamond-shaped courtyard, the school has become an oversized symbol of the achievement gap.

A 2006 New York City Department of Education "Quality Review Report" gave the school failing grades on even the most basic functions of education, including monitoring student progress. The report noted that "school safety was a major issue, and considerable time was spent in establishing a calm, safe, and orderly environment."(One former student commented that "the kids are sooooooo bad. The police is always there.") Not surprisingly, few students passed the state Regents exam, and, according to the New York State School Report Card for the 2007–2008 school year, only a single student in the entire graduating class reported plans to attend a two- or four-year college. (The school graduated its final class at the end of the 2009–2010 school year.)

The Brooklyn Generation School is only biting off a small piece of the job of educating the city's poorly served students, but early results show strides. In the 2008–2009 school year, although 59 percent of African American students (87 percent of the student body) entered the school performing in the lowest third of students citywide, the school earned a "value added" score of 1.7 in Global Studies and Math (any score above 1.0 represents progress in closing the achievement gap).

When students at the end of tenth grade took two Regents exams, 70 percent passed Global Studies and more than 60 percent passed the Integrated Algebra exam; about 54 percent passed both and another 17 percent almost passed, scoring 55 to 64, with 65 being the minimum passing score. By contrast, just 44 percent of students at the traditional South Shore High School passed Global Studies and 17 percent passed Math. And in another key measure that is often underplayed, students earning at least ten course credits per year toward graduation, 80 percent of first-year and 72 percent of second-year Brooklyn Generation Students hit that target, above the city mean of 75 and 70 percent of students. The results were more dramatic among those who entered the school in the lowest third academically, as 75 percent of those second-year Brooklyn Generation students in 2008–2009 earned ten credits toward on-time graduation, compared with 55 percent of their peers citywide.

The school has not yet graduated its first class, but it is attracting attention for its approach of mixing innovation with district requirements (including union contracts and budgets) to give students more hours and more tailored instruction. "I do think we need new models," says urban school reformer Ellen Guiney, executive director of the Boston Plan for Excellence, a nonprofit with business support dedicated to backing school improvement. In watching more than a quarter-century of reform efforts come and go, she appreciates that Generation Schools leaders are rethinking time and course structures to give students more support and time with adults. Her experience in Boston's school reform effort, which has had challenges as well as some successes, has taught her that despite lofty talk, there are certain realities that innovators must work with. "As a practical matter, you are not going to change the teaching force in urban education overnight. You can grab all the good teachers and put them in three or four schools, but what is that going to do?" she says. "I do think using the teachers we have in more flexible ways and somewhat different ways is important. We need more collective embracing of each kid and groups of teachers sharing the progress of the kids . . . We need to have models that can figure out what each kid needs."

Progress, but Not Enough

There are a lot of good and new ideas being tried in urban schools these days. Not all of them work. One characteristic of this moment in education reform is, for good or ill, an impatience for results. Some of this is the well-intentioned recognition that children's lives are passing and that we must have better schools immediately. Some pressure is political, to show that those in charge, in whom the public has trusted, are honoring that trust and recording progress. And then there is the fact that we are trying to make up, perhaps too quickly, for long-entrenched failed practices. So while we may see indications of success, the nature of broad-scale reform means that some schools may get better—but not better enough.

There is plenty of vocal support for closing schools that don't raise student scores. As a policy position, this makes perfect sense. Why perpetuate mediocrity? But there is a gap between the policy idea and the reality of shutting down a school—not in theory but in what happens in that slow-motion period when everyone knows the end is coming. Like collateral damage in a military offensive, there is a price for shutting a school. This is not to suggest that a school should not be closed but, rather, that we be mindful that closure is itself an educational direction that needs a process to ensure that students' learning time is not wasted. In frank terms, should a child have to repeat kindergarten because the teacher was absent for virtually the *entire* year? In the compact of public trust, where does that leave turnaround?

The Dr. Ramon E. Betances School was closed at the end of the 2009–2010 school year, redesigned, and reopened in the fall of 2010 as an early literacy lab school. But during the 2009–2010 school year, the real challenge for acting principal Karen Gray was how to push ahead a school that is about to shut down, as well as how to manage the emotions and practical matters, such as ensuring teachers still show up for work and students still make academic progress.

Gray remembered that it was Thursday, September 17, 2009, when she received the message from the school secretary that Christina Kishimoto, assistant superintendent for school design, wanted to talk. Gray, thinking that they were in the midst of a self-directed redesign in which it was up to them to improve student scores (and they were working on it) to avoid district takeover, was excited. But no. In short order, Gray got a different message: the school was being closed. Instead of being a neighborhood elementary school, it would be reopened the following September as the Betances Early Reading Lab School, serving grades K–3. The entire staff would be let go, and everyone would have to reapply for their jobs. Gray looked at the job description for the new principal. "It doesn't look like it was written for me," she observed, sitting in the principal's office several months after the news and obviously uncertain what her future would hold as a thirty-three-year-old who had specifically committed herself to a career in urban education, no less.

There is *no way*, given the parameters that Hartford superintendent Steven Adamowski set out, that Betances would be considered a success. Students taking state tests in reading, writing, and math were performing far below their state and even their district peers. In the 2008–2009 academic year, only 9.8 percent of fourth graders reached proficiency in reading, compared with 74.4 percent statewide (and 36.8 percent districtwide). By fifth grade, slightly more than half reached proficiency in math, one-fourth in reading, and less than a third in writing (statewide figures are 86, 77, and 86 percent, respectively). In Adamowski's matrix, Betances was in the red (dark gray in table 2.1).

But while it seems like a straightforward decision to close a poorly performing school, the facts on the ground are more nuanced. The school is located in a neighborhood of housing projects, and across the street is a home for kids with emotional challenges that make them difficult to place in foster homes. Wherever they have come from, whenever they have arrived, they simply cross the street. This was their school. Gray, however, understood the numbers and expectations: "I know Dr. Adamowski's mission. I know there is a criteria. I knew if XYZ doesn't happen that, although you are making changes, you don't meet the standard the changes will be made for you." Gray, in other words, got the agenda. Unfortunately, she was the one in the middle of it. As someone who came to the school four years earlier, who, given the vagaries of school budgets, had been pink-slipped and rehired multiple times, Gray was left to lead a school that was trying to be better even as teachers discovered their jobs would cease to exist at the end of the academic year.

After getting the news from Kishimoto, Gray held an emergency staff meeting. Kishimoto visited the school to personally share the news a few days later. At that meeting there were tears and anger. The school *had* made strides; while the 3 percent per year improvement the school had registered was below the target 4 percent, there was progress of other sorts. When she arrived, says Gray, it was a chaotic and dangerous place. Students were constantly suspended. One teacher recounted finding a crack pipe on a kindergartner and having a parent accuse her of planting it. Ambulances were called on a regular basis to deal with emotionally out-of-control children. "People will tell you stories about children crawling out of windows. No academic work was going on," she said. By midpoint in the 2009–2010 year, by contrast, she had called an ambulance only twice, and both times for medical situations. The walls of her office were covered in charts recording student academic progress by grade, subject, and teacher. "When I came here four years ago, it was not about data, it was about survival. It was about making sure no one will get hurt," she said.

Schools like Betances have the task of teaching, even as students arrive from homes wrought with unfathomable problems. It *does* feel like progress to present them with stability. Yet that's clearly not enough. This exposes a frustrating issue: while no one wants to expect less from the most challenging cases, it's obvious that some high-poverty schools are harder to turn around than others. This is not to seek or demand less but to understand that the poor inner city is not one homogeneous mass but its own geography of needs requiring specific engagements.

Despite poor test scores and troubled home lives, Betances is orderly and quiet on a January day. Children walk in lines with their lunch trays. They wear uniforms; they care enough about authority to mistakenly worry that being called to the principal's office to speak with a reporter means that they are getting in trouble. Yet somewhere between such progress and an imagined ideal—or what policy makers and leaders believe is a reasonable expectation of public education in America—is a school that is a safe haven but is ineffective. Shutting down Betances can well be read as compelling evidence of legitimate progress and commitment to a goal. But closure itself has consequences: it is a messy process in a fragile setting.

The Fallout of Shutdown

During the emergency staff meeting in September, Gray reassured teachers, as best she could, that just because they must reapply for a job at the school doesn't mean they won't be hired. After all, as a staff they had done professional development with Haskins Laboratories, a nonprofit institute (affiliated with Yale and the University of Connecticut) focused on using research to improve reading interventions. That would seem to make these teachers attractive to a principal building a school focused on reading and literacy. But her more immediate message was, "The children are still in front of us. We have made commitments. We will walk out of here with our head held high—and our scores will reflect that," she says, pausing from recounting the talk to collect her emotions. "I am getting teary."

Months later, in January, some teachers had taken her words to heart and were working hard. First-grade teacher Kathryn McEachern, who graduated from Trinity College in 2007, started her master's degree, still tutored students after school, and continued to push her students to achieve. She had eighteen in her class, and, with the exception of a boy who arrived from Puerto Rico a few weeks before we spoke, she said proudly, "they all can read." January of first grade—not bad. McEachern, who was offered a higher-paying job in a suburban community as a literacy coordinator just weeks before she learned of the Betances closure, was half-kicking herself for turning down a secure job for an uncertain future. But she also believes in her ability to help these kids and was working to be rehired. "I am doing everything in my power so that when it comes to reapply, they would be crazy not to take me," she said.

She decided not to discuss the closing with her students, preferring to keep her focus on the work. There were things she could do, she says, that would matter to her students well beyond first grade. That is why rules in her classroom seemed to be as much about parenting and character development as classroom management (although they certainly go together). She had rules about telling the truth, asking before touching or hugging, not calling out, and being respectful. She believes in planning and order. "I give them stability in my classroom. I keep them on a schedule every day. They know when things are coming up. I give them lots of responsibility."

Not every teacher, however, responded to the closure in this way.

Gray says three teachers were absent more than usual, with two teachers in particular together missing 27 percent of the school year to that point. And the absence of a kindergarten teacher who had been out on a medical leave, who was expected back after Christmas but extended the leave again, meant that they hired serial substitutes. By January, students in that class had their regular teacher for only twenty-one school days—a little over three weeks, making it likely, observed Gray, that many students would need to repeat kindergarten—"and it's not their fault."

What made Gray most upset about the teachers who repeatedly called in sick was that without money in the budget for daily substitutes, students were "dispersed" to other classrooms. The practice was frequent enough that *dispersed* was no mere vocabulary list selection but part of the lexicon common throughout the school—as in, "I'm being dispersed." On one January day, an entire class of fifth graders was tucked into the backs of various grade classrooms, playing educational games on the computer and chatting among themselves, waiting for lunch, for recess, for the school day to end with little of substance accomplished. Fifth grader José Jimenez spoke up during an interview to say he liked being dispersed because it meant more free time and, in one first-grade classroom, he got to pass out papers. "I get to help the teacher," he said, unaware that his time is being wasted.

While do-no-work time draws only mild objections from grade school kids, for the other teachers it is downright frustrating. "We are all disappointed" about the closing, said third-grade teacher Yvonne D'Eliseo. "But this is my job. There are a few who for whatever reason have just given up. They don't come into work quite a lot and their students get dispersed into other classrooms, and I know it is just because they have a negative attitude," she says. "You can't be sick twice a week every week." And while students were supposed to come with a folder of assigned work to complete, they rarely did. "I'll try to scrounge up something I might have, but I don't know the student's ability. It kills me that they are sitting there doing nothing."

Doing nothing for so much of the school year meant that students like José who wants to fix cars one day, lose ground academically. Students in grades 3, 4, and 5 took benchmark math tests in September and in December. While students in grades 3 and 4 made gains (from 38 percent to a stunning 835 percent, an eight-plus-fold improvement) in reaching proficiency levels, students in the two fifth-grade classes in which teachers have been chronically absent saw their scores actually drop by 24 and 30 percent.

And while Gray tried to push forward, a kind of resolute sadness had settled over the school by January. She required every teacher to take charge of a hallway bulletin board to display student work or create data walls showing student progress. But after one teacher simply stapled up several rows of photocopied math sheets, Gray asked her to take it down. That's not what she meant by "student work." As Gray strolled down the fifth grade hallway, one teacher's room empty because she was absent and students were dispersed, she paused before a large expanse of yellow and pink construction paper with scalloped borders. It displayed nothing. "I don't believe everyone wants to do a great job," said Gray. "I am not pro or against unions, but to move a tenured teacher out is moving mountains." She estimated that it may be only 5 to 10 percent of the teaching workforce that is falling down on the job, but school closure brings things to the surface. "It isn't a lot—except when you have twenty-five students in front of them," she said referring to the two absent fifth-grade teachers. "That's when you have fifty students who are getting ineffective teachers for 180 days."

4

SUITS, COWBOYS,
AND SURROGATE MOMS

SHARON JOHNSON NEVER PLANNED TO BE a principal, much less one known for inner-city success. Yet, before Steve Adamowski tapped her in 2002 to lead Withrow University High School as part of Cincinnati's high school restructuring effort, she had taken Parham Elementary School from being among the district's worst performers to, just two years later, the verge of being among the best. Gains in test scores (fourth-grade writing, for example, rose twenty-four points) earned her praise and a visit in 2000 from U.S. Department of Education secretary Richard Riley.

When Johnson took over Withrow University High School, only half of the city's high school students were earning diplomas. By 2007–2008, its graduation rate was 97.7 percent (the district average was 82.9 percent, and the Ohio state average was 84.6 percent). One of three smaller schools formed out of the old Withrow High School and located on a stately collegelike campus, Withrow University High School has become such a popular pick in the city's choice system that Elizabeth Holtzapple, the district's director of research, evaluation, and test administration, says that Withrow is now over its design capacity of 600 (enrollment is 750) and always has a waiting list. (It didn't help that *U.S. News and World Report* in 2007 put Withrow University

High on its "bronze medal" list in its first-ever ranking of the best public high schools in the United States.)

The challenge of taking a failing school and shaping it into a successful small high school whose student population is 96 percent African American and 60 percent "economically disadvantaged" drives Johnson in a way she could never have imagined. "I have a passion for this stuff," she says. "I love this. Never thought I would. I am glad someone saw something in me, because I don't think I would have ever seen it in myself."

Help Wanted: Extreme Leadership

Johnson's assertions that it took someone else to spot her leadership ability and that she wouldn't have picked this path for herself reveal some of the difficulty districts have in finding principals who can lead school-level turnaround: it's not always clear who will be good. In the past, principals didn't need the same skills as they do now. This is not to suggest that there haven't been tremendous school leaders, but there are new pressures and skills required of turnaround principals. Rather than being caretakers, they must be agents of change. The job is not about preserving but about dismantling failed patterns and practices— and doing it in a way that doesn't feel disruptive but affirmative.

Effective school leaders can have very different styles, strengths, and approaches, but, at the same time, they share a constellation of qualities that makes them productive. They understand their school, their students, and their parents. They understand the goal and where they are in relation to that goal. They are willing to do things differently, even if it means risking criticism. They lean on others. In other words, they are part CEO, armed with research, plans, data targets, and checkpoints; part cowboy, doing what needs doing and asking questions (or forgiveness) later; and part surrogate mom, touching students and teachers in a way that raises each individual's game and encourages risks and collective actions that yield success.

The composite image of suit/cowboy/mom (which is not meant to be gender specific) describes leaders who have a focus, energy, and spirit about them that acknowledge the hard work of turnaround without letting up. Such leaders are compelling to others. They are not confused about what matters or what they are trying to accomplish. They have excellent common sense. They are ambitious but also realistic and grounded regarding practical concerns and the implications of those concerns on larger goals. They manage to "sweat the small stuff" without becoming overwhelmed by it (often with the help of a key person whom they trust). They build a culture that others want to be a part of. They can separate what schools do—the effort—from the result, the effect. Just because teachers are trying doesn't mean students are actually learning. These leaders care about the "product" of schooling from the consumer end—What is the experience like? How is it working? What do we do well? Where are we coming up short?

Leading Like It's Family

Even though Sharon Johnson led the turnaround of Withrow University High School beginning in 2002 in a somewhat different climate from what we have today, there are strong lessons to be learned from her approach. There is, after all, timeless value in her commonsense leadership style. As a one-time single mother who worried about paying bills and buying food, Johnson understands that home pressures complicate student learning. Recognizing that many of her students were coming from homes rife with stresses and dysfunctional relationships, Johnson built her turnaround on the belief that school success was more likely if students were well cared for. From the start she has sought to provide students an environment that offers stability, guidance, and support. For her, the school is a kind of family, and she uses that metaphor frequently.

She also understands that details matter, especially to teens. This is why Johnson keeps a closet of extra clothing and even a washer and dryer for students who need laundry help. It's why the day before we spoke she had visited a student's home after noticing the girl, a junior, suddenly struggling in classes. "I wanted to speak with her parents because something was happening in her world," says Johnson, who discovered that a parent had lost a job. "There was not a whole lot of food at the house, and she didn't have bus fare. We can fix the bus fare. We can get some food at the house. I cannot pay the bills. A school can only do so much. But my philosophy is, 'Let me do everything I can do.'"

This may sound more like social work than education, but Johnson is not sure that in urban schools you can have one without the other. Her successes at Parham and Withrow have been helped by strong connections with community agencies that provide support for her students and families. The social service agency, Families Forward, has social workers connected with the school, reinforcing her belief that students' home lives are her concern. And students feel this. In the district's May 2009 student survey, three-fourths of Withrow University High ninth and eleventh graders surveyed answered "yes" when asked, "Does your principal know who you are?" Only 46 percent of their student peers districtwide could say the same.

What's striking about Johnson's involvement in students' home lives is that she is at once pragmatic—sending a student to the showers if she thinks he needs to bathe—while also careful not to be judgmental. "Parents are sending us what they have. It is our job to make them the best we can. That encompasses having counseling moments. It encompasses motherly advice, life skills. It includes, 'What do I do if you come to school with a smell?'" says Johnson. "We can't fix home, but I can fix things here."

Using Single-Sex Classes to Support Family Culture

One controversial thing Johnson did when she became principal of Withrow was to separate academic courses into single-sex classes. Boys and girls attend school together, eat together in the cafeteria, and participate together in afterschool tutoring and extracurricular activities. But their academics are separate. This approach nearly doomed the project amid worries that single-sex classes would spur lawsuits, says Joe Nathan, director of the Center for School Change at Macalester College, who helped guide the district during the Gates Foundation–supported high school restructuring. But Nathan says district leaders heard from top federal education officials that "they would love to see some schools trying this."

At the time, only sixteen public schools in the nation conducted girls-only and boys-only classes, a number that has soared since the U.S. Department of Education in 2006 issued regulations allowing single-sex classes in public schools. As of February 2010, according to the National Association for Single-Sex Public Education, there were 540 schools in the United States holding single-sex classes. While supporters of single-sex education often cite a range of beliefs about differences in learning styles between the sexes and questionable arguments about different brain structures, leaving a mixed body of research (that sometimes comes off as advocacy), Johnson wasn't seeking to engage arguments about gender differences. Rather, she wanted to use the structure of sex-separate classes to carve some social and educational breathing space for students.

Johnson says the single-sex core classes—electives like art, journalism, and other classes are coed—help reinforce her goal of building a "family culture" at Withrow. Each summer before school begins, and at various times throughout the year, she reinforces this family setting by breaking students into all-male and all-female discussion groups. Johnson says they talk about character and social issues, problems, and gender-specific worries. "How do you deal with death?" asks Johnson, citing an example. "We do a lot of things you would normally do at home." Both girls and boys are more vocal and frank about personal struggles and issues in a single-sex setting, she says, pointing out that helping kids work through these matters—giving them the skills and a place to seek support—benefits their academic work as well.

Support, Accountability, and Collaboration

Johnson's quest for a family-style environment extends to the school's professional culture. She promotes give-and-take and, in fact, every two years has staff evaluate her leadership and provide feedback. This tone also feeds a culture in which teachers are expected to troubleshoot, problem-solve, and collaborate. "We set goals in this building," she says. "We are all accountable for making things happen. The attitude is, 'We are a family—so let's talk about it.'"

This, however, does not mean that teachers are not rigorously evaluated. It may be all the rage in reform right now, but Johnson had already been tracking student test results by teacher. "You've got to personalize it," she says, noting that at staff meetings she will put up PowerPoint slides showing how teachers in a department perform compared with one another according to student test scores. If one is outperforming another, Johnson guides a discussion: "What is Miss Allison doing better in her classroom than Miss Young?" That, says Johnson, "is how teachers learn. One might have 90 and one 91—that's nothing to talk about. Having your work put up front, there is nothing wrong with that. It's like a company: these are the results."

While Johnson admits that "at first they didn't like it," she has seen teacher opposition turn to department-focused support. Science, for example, has been a weak area in terms of student test scores (only 69.8 percent of tenth graders at Withrow passed the science graduation test in 2008–2009 compared with 76 percent statewide, according to the state report card). Johnson says science teachers have started working together more intensely. "The science department has said, 'We are sick of you riding us.' Every department wants to shine."

Dr. Gloria Ononye is head of Withrow's science department and says her department is collaborating to tackle student performance. They have collectively reworked parts of the curriculum, says Ononye, noting that they are trying to make up for elementary and middle school years in which students received little science training. They are also trying to keep students moving forward. In concrete terms, she says, teachers will step into one another's classrooms to help out. The day before we spoke, Ononye worked with a group of students in her colleague's biology class to help with a prelab because they had been absent when it was done in class. This enabled them to catch up and, later in the period, join the rest of the class in doing the lab, which was about how different factors affect plant growth. That was during the first bell, she said. "A chemistry teacher was free the last bell so she came and did the same thing I did," says Ononye. "We are not exactly where we want to be, but you have to make incremental progress."

Johnson's Tool: Keen Observations

Johnson cares about relationships, but she also cares about data and results. Her philosophy is simple: "If the teachers are not producing, the kids will not produce." While Johnson believes it is a school leader's job to mentor, model, and teach, she also spends a lot of time simply observing. "I study my people," she says. "We do retreats. We take the whole staff away from the city and you get to know who your leaders are, who your whiners are, who your followers are. You use that time to look strategically for leadership in that group; you look for positive people."

She has individual meetings with each of the fifty teachers in her building to find out what their concerns and struggles are, "so we have a relationship and we can build trust." She also walks through hallways and classrooms, taking note: "I am out and looking at them. I am looking at their facial expressions. I can tell when they are sick and when a teacher is not having a good day."

Johnson's close scrutiny dates to her childhood when she would visit her mother's elementary school classroom in Warner Robins, Georgia. Her mother, now retired, taught both second and third grade, and Johnson recalls noticing how her mother's approach was different from her own teacher's methods. "My mother made sure every child in her classroom understood what she taught for the day. She made time to give every child individualized attention. I didn't see that at my school. I was eight years old and I noticed that."

Working in an inner-city high school can wear you down, which is why Johnson tries to balance bottom-line demands with empathy. "I know teachers get tired," she says. Her talent is getting the most and best from people, and one of her strategies is to keep teachers motivated by providing positive feedback in the form of the notes she writes each teacher, one at least every other month. The notes are based on things she notices. "I tell them, 'I know you are tired, but I see you pushing.'" Says Johnson, "If I walk into a classroom and they are up on their feet and moving from kid to kid—that is everything."

While Johnson is supportive and complementary when a teacher is working effectively, she is direct when someone is flagging. "I have this teacher I am dealing with right now," she says. "He is up at the board. He calls it 'teaching.' I call it 'covering the material.' When you are teaching, they learn; when you cover it, you are exposing them to the material. That is what I have been on this teacher about." She has looked at the formative and summative assessments of his students and gone through his grade book, noting the number of students who are failing his tests. Such pressure, she says, often makes poor-performing teachers decide to move on. "I heard he is already looking," she says, with a tone of satisfaction. "He is new and he doesn't want to work that hard. This school is not for every teacher. Everyone is not cut out to be in an urban school."

Good Leaders Are Hard to Find

As superintendent in Cincinnati, Steven Adamowski spotted natural leadership ability in Sharon Johnson and tapped her to lead a turnaround effort at a time when this was a more novel idea than it is now. Today, the press to fix a lot of poorly performing schools—quickly—requires many Sharon Johnson–like principals. And, says Adamowski, there just aren't enough. In Hartford, for example, he says they have about a dozen vacancies a year in principalships and a difficult time recruiting top candidates. Certainly, some cities are more attractive places to live, which makes it easier to lure talent. In Hartford, the job of screening principals falls to Christina Kishimoto, assistant superintendent for school design. Too often, appealing candidates tell her that they "love what you are doing in Hartford" but don't want to live there themselves.

Kishimoto is frank about the challenges in hiring: "Our pool is weak. We have an applicant pool that has little experience in administrative ranks." While many teachers move from classroom to administration, guessing who will be great and who will flop is not easy. Mistakes are made. In the 2009–2010 school year, Kishimoto replaced principals in one new turnaround school and restructured leadership in another because they were failing. "We went with individuals who were strong in the classroom but were found not to have the administrative skills. Even with support they were struggling. Their vision and their intent is there, but they were struggling to deliver."

Adamowski says reform calls for different kinds of people to become principals than districts required in the past. "A key factor is you need people who are entrepreneurial, who view this as running their own enterprise." Adamowski believes principals need strong content knowledge and a small business mind-set. "The rest," he says, "they can learn."

Charter School Lesson: Grow the Principals You Want

It is stunningly difficult to find ready-made leaders who can drive building-level change in urban schools. This isn't helped by the maddening fact that, despite efforts to identify possible core competencies of school-level turnaround leaders, it remains too much of a mystery as to who will actually succeed. Increasingly, it is becoming clear that districts have to do more themselves: if you can't find great principals, it may make sense to grow them yourself. Because the nation's best-performing charter schools have strong and unique school cultures that are central to their identities, it has made sense from the start to train, rather than uncover, individuals to lead their schools.

A common approach is to understand and clearly define the institutional culture, find individuals who are like-minded, and, over time, develop school-level leaders. This reflects a key difference in how districts and charters approach personnel, both teachers and school leaders. Where districts expect leaders to get most of their training outside and bring it into the system, charters put significant resources into fostering leadership from within, in part because the very specific leadership they want simply isn't out there (and, to be fair, many of their hires are young and do not come with previous training).

"We *have* to grow our own leaders," says Dacia Toll, cofounder of charter school network Achievement First. Toll says they devote a lot of resources to identifying and bringing along talent. For example, Achievement First has teams of full-time recruiters whose job is to identify and vet teacher candidates, including those who will become part of their future leadership pipeline. Every Achievement First school leader also has a coach and a "Professional Growth Plan," a thirteen-page internal document that includes detailed assessment checklists that require submission of student test data and evidence to support assertions.

It also includes a self-assessment and outside evaluation by a coach on broad leadership goals as well as subcategories that ensure, for example, that there are systematic interventions when a student struggles and that teachers keep in mind the importance of attending to the "J-Factor for Students and Families"—that is, joy factor. How well, for example, does the leader make sure the school is a place "where it is 'cool' to be smart" and where "students and parents have fun along the journey up the mountain"? The aim, says Toll, is not to have every leader perfect in every category but to provide a framework for evaluation, face-to-face feedback and goal setting, to help them become better leaders (the document is edited and rewritten following meetings between the school leader and a coach). The point is that learning to lead is a growth process that benefits from feedback and self-reflection.

At KIPP's national network of charter schools, spokesman Steve Mancini says they spend a full year training a school leader before that person steps into the post (training pay ranges from $60,000 to $80,000, depending on the average principal pay in the region where they are located). The training includes coursework at a Leadership Institute at New York University, hands-on residencies at KIPP schools, and a "boot camp" at which they work through details of planning and running a school before beginning work on their own with guidance from a team.

The Knowledge Is Power Program, however, has made an important adjustment to its leadership model since the first school opened in 1994. "We originally had the view of the 'one heroic leader,'" says Mancini. Today, KIPP structures its schools to employ what he calls "a more distributive leadership." Mancini says that while there is a school head, they now have "two lieutenants below the captain." In some schools, lieutenant-level leaders split responsibilities either according to grade levels (one handling grades 5 and 6 and the other 7 and 8) or by operations and academics. The lieutenant leaders also receive training. As a result, a school's leadership team has all been through similar training, thereby helping them work together.

So while district schools may have assistant principals and teacher leaders, what KIPP brings to the equation is the value of a uniform training approach and a strong shared-power structure among a school's top administrators. This allows for a succession plan and a way to sustain programs and quality. "When we started off, it was 'train the founder and that is enough,'" says Mancini. "But we learned the life cycle of the founder is about seven years. If your founder leaves, you want to be able to pivot an assistant principal into that role."

Intuitively, the idea makes sense. And increasingly districts are recognizing the need to have a hand in training their brand of school leader. In Hartford the district formed a committee to identify and support new leaders as well as create better support and professional development for existing school leaders. This move recognizes that school turnaround demands special skills and that principals may need help acquiring them. The district partnered with Travelers Insurance Company and launched a Leadership Academy that in August 2010 was poised to recruit its first three leaders to, in KIPP style, spend a year doing leadership training, including spending time with a supervisory principal. Despite such initiatives, much of school turnaround leadership is far from a well-grooved road. Urban school principals more often than not are reaching deep into themselves to lead in a way they hope will turn around their schools—and their student's lives.

Lead Like Your Hair Is on Fire

It is much too early to tell if High School, Inc., one of Hartford's newest small turnaround high schools that opened in September 2009 as an insurance and finance academy, will be successful. But principal Terrell Hill is not a guy you want to bet against. A self-described "inner-city kid" who was raised, along with his brother, by a single mother in Springfield, Massachusetts, public housing and is now a dissertation away from his doctorate, is the embodiment of streetwise pragmatism, drive, and big vision.

As he strolls around his school, which is located in a downtown Hartford office building across from the XL Center, where the University of Connecticut women and men's basketball teams play, he points out that the reception area is designed to be like a business office to help acclimate students. There is a credit union branch next door where Hill hopes students can someday have paid internships. Like many offices, the school has a workout room but no athletics program, though Hill wants to start golf and tennis. "The sports that business people play," he says. "Every kid in Hartford knows what a basketball court looks like. We need to expose them to something different."

On a sunny, crisp winter day less than six months after the school's opening, Hill shows off a library that is empty except for some donated books in boxes. He talks about plans for flat screens and stock tickers. He proudly points out the school's crest—a shield with the words *in-*

dustry and *integrity* modeled on his high school alma mater's—that is stamped on a thumb drive that each student is issued. He wants kids to own those values.

As teens shuffle through the hallways and a top student named Denise stops, at his request, to show off the gold honors pin on her blazer lapel, it appears some students are buying in. But while Denise and her freshman classmates are embracing High School, Inc.'s culture, Hill has his hands full with the sophomores. The tenth graders, he says, were just tested, and only four of the sixty-five are reading beyond the ninth-grade level. "Most of these kids are like lower middle school, upper elementary school, fifth to eighth grade," he says. "Part of me is just trying to figure out who do I have."

At a citywide choice fair several weeks earlier, Hill had the task of introducing his school to prospective parents and students. Even as he tries to get his new school in order—which involves, among other things, massaging relationships with city business leaders like Travelers Insurance, a key supporter—Hill needs to think about where his next year's ninth-grade class will come from. He needs to enroll 100 new freshmen, and, given the challenges of showing test result success, he, like Adam Johnson at Hartford Public High School's Law and Government Academy, wants good students—or, more accurately, students who will work hard. "I don't want to get into the creaming game," Hill says. "I don't need to have all the kids who get straight As. I need students who will work to their ability and parents who will be supportive."

This sounds simpler than it is. One of Hill's greatest leadership challenges is to set a tone of expectation for students and parents in a culture in which little has been asked of them in the past. At one point in the late fall, he called sixty parents to come to the school for a meeting. They were parents of students "who needed some focus and attention." Only fourteen showed. While the turnout was disappointing, Hill began what would become something of a drumbeat and a mark of his leadership style: accountability—not just for the school, because Adamowski's office would be all over that, but for the students and the parents.

In an approach very different from Sharon Johnson's at Withrow University High School, Hill was blunt in his message to parents, telling them they needed to intervene and get their teens working. "I wasn't telling them, 'You need to leave,'" he insists. "I'm telling them that 'this is the standard at High School, Inc., and it's not going to move.' I do what I do and it works. I said to parents, 'You are doing what you are doing and it's not working.'" Hill says that "there will be some kids who will get lost. I said to parents, 'I will not quit on your kid. You and your kids will quit on me. We are putting out a product. It is here if you want it.'"

This is tough talk, but Hill believes that if his students are to have the opportunities he and his right-hand man, David Gay, the school's business director, are working to create, they need to represent quality. "Branding is important." In urban settings, Hill insists, too many principals shrink from being frank with parents. "I know these parents want the best for their kids, but they don't know how to get there. They know what it looks like—the house and the car—but no one has been honest with them since day one," he says. "I tell the parents, 'I am trying to give your kids the same thing I am giving my daughters.'"

Like many people, Hill leads from his personal history. One doesn't get very far in a conversation with him without hearing about his mother. "She is my hero," he says. Growing up in public housing, Hill recalls that by fourth grade many of his friends "went the other way." "I was in classes with all white kids," he says. His mother insisted he and his brother work hard—no excuses. "My mother spoke to us, 'You got a B? You could have gotten an A. She used to tell me when I was five years old, 'When you are in school, you are competing.'"

The hard work and lessons that come from educating yourself out of poverty, together with the belief that the inner city is best lifted by those who live there, drive Hill in both his dealings with parents and in his larger mission of changing the trajectory of as many lives as he can. For someone who has been the only black teacher in a high school as well as a suburban principal, trying his hand at inner city reform is particularly appealing. His own history also makes him push a little harder and with a little more urgency. He describes one conversation with a mother of a tenth grader who reads at a sixth-grade level. Hill sat down with the boy's mother and warned her that her son "was headed for disaster." He put it plainly: "He is a big black male who is not performing academically. You guys need to decide what you want. You and I both know what will happen to him. He isn't a gangster, but he is always in the middle of something." A principal who is white or perhaps from a different background would find it difficult to speak that way. "I am very much aware of that," says Hill. "And I use it."

Getting It Done

As much as Hill demands of students, he is also demanding of himself. His leadership is not just about prodding others but about solving problems and getting things done—even if that means painting walls and hanging SMART Boards on a Saturday or standing in the rain in the parking lot of Buffalo Wild Wings to recruit an English teacher as she waits for her husband to pick up takeout (she's now in room 309).

Like other forward-thinking districts, Hartford wants to encourage dramatic change but has not eliminated bureaucratic holdups and union issues that make reform wait its turn. Sometimes, especially with the turnaround clock ticking, leaders need to be rule breakers, or benders. That approach precisely suits Hill, who says he read all twelve union contracts (from school district carpenters to teachers) to understand how best to make the system work for him. How, in other words, could he hire a key leadership team member from outside the district? What would that position have to look like? In the end, Gay came on as business director and plays a key role. He has organized thirty-eight volunteer tutors from the business community to work with students during study halls and has five business leaders lined up to come in and talk about ethics. As subtle and demure as Hill is forward, Gay manages the school's relationships with business partners and seeks out internship opportunities for students. But Gay's job is not all glamour; he also spends time tracking down ever-changing and elusive parent cell phone numbers. He buys into Hill's intense, hands-on approach. "One of the things that brought me here was Terrell—his integrity," says Gay.

That integrity, however, is not about rule following when, say, Hill needed electrical outlets installed in eighteen classrooms. According to him, the official quote from the school district would have required time-and-a-half pay and two electricians and a supervisor, cutting into his budget by some $5,000. "Eighteen outlets? I could get all that done in one working Saturday!" complained Hill, who contacted a contractor he knew and had it done for $2,300—"less than half!" He took a similar approach to hanging the SMART Boards in his classrooms, paying his custodians to help him do the job rather than submitting a request downtown. "I paid my custodians, plus we hung out together on a Saturday doing it," says Hill. "I said, 'Guys, it is one metal bracket with five screws. I'll bring my laser level.' And they learned a new skill."

That same pragmatism extends to guiding the students at High School, Inc. He clearly wants them to do more than pass state tests. He wants to give them experiences to help lift them into the middle class, including teaching the social skills that entrance requires. For example, students like Denise who make the honor roll and receive gold lapel pins and certificates are also invited to lunch. "I made an announcement over the PA, 'All honor roll students please report to the main lobby. We are about to leave for our honor lunch.'" Hill calls the lunch he arranged in a private dining room at Hot Tomato's Restaurant down the street an "executive lunch." When they arrive at the restaurant, a nice place, some students, he says, are tentative and nervous. They wonder if they may ask for another Sprite or more bread. The answer is an emphatic *Yes!* But even at lunch Hill is pushing. There is a lesson he wants students to take away from the experience: "There is a benefit to working hard. You will go to lunch at places like this." He wants them "to understand that this is clearly all within their grasp."

Leading Before Turnaround: One Principal, Two Schools

With Hartford's Bellizzi Middle School in disarray with poor performance and losing pupils, Stacey McCann was tapped as a kind of pre-turnaround principal. For the past five years, she has also been principal of the preK–5 Henry C. Dwight Elementary School that is around the corner from Bellizzi. The two schools were merged beginning in the 2010–2011 school year, forming the Dwight-Bellizzi Asian Studies Academy (a K–8 school). McCann, having been charged with leading two starkly different schools and staffs—and, yes, with trying to bring them together—began critical work during the 2009–2010 school year.

In a premerger interview one winter afternoon in McCann's Dwight office, the challenge was obvious. Even as she tried to carry on a conversation, her walkie-talkie crackled with dispatches from Bellizzi, including problems typical in urban schools that are adrift. (At one point later in the day, a girl refused to go home on the school bus because another girl said she would stab her if she did. The first girl claimed to have seen a weapon. The question: Could someone come by and supervise a search?)

Despite the chaos of the situation and the surroundings, Dwight felt like a learning wonderland. No matter that the building was 127 years old, that bathrooms were all the way down in the basement, or that the heat was funky. There were decorative stars and mortarboards dangling on gold Mylar curls from the ceiling, and there was no surface that was not adorned with student work. There were uplifting quotations from famous people like Rembrandt and Cicero. An orange laminated poster conveyed information worth knowing, such as wage comparisons by education level (for example, less than a high school degree gets you $21,391; a professional law or medical degree yields you $80,230). Outside each classroom door was a sign noting what year students inside the classroom will attend college. A display opposite the office reminded students of behavioral goals not of the general sort but explicit instructions on how to interact politely with others. When I visited, the week's

93

focus was "Having a conversation" and "Using appropriate voice tone." And this was not just so much filler decoration; every interaction with building staff felt like they had studied up on the polite conversation lesson. The security staff was friendly and helpful ("Are you looking for the office?"). In the teachers' lounge, it was someone's birthday, and the retired security officer who volunteers at the school every day had made a coconut cake. *Was this for real?*

What's essential to know is that it is more than feel-good shtick. While Bellizzi was, alas, at the bottom row in "intervention" red on Adamowski's color-coded matrix, Dwight was at the very top in "autonomous" spring green. Although it was in a poor immigrant neighborhood (95 percent of students received free or reduced-price lunches, 29 percent were not fluent in English, and only half of the parents spoke English), Dwight was one of the five highest-achieving schools in the district and was the only non–magnet school to have reached the district goal of a 70 OSI score.

The achievement gulf between Dwight and Bellizzi was illustrated dramatically in October 2009 when about a hundred staff from both schools gathered for their regular staff meeting. It was the same day the district issued bonus checks to staff at fourteen schools that were either among the district's top performers or that had made significant improvement. "It just happened to be a staff meeting day, so I passed them out," says McCann. Each Dwight teacher received $2,500, and each Dwight staff member received $1,250; Bellizzi teachers and staff received nothing. "My teachers at Dwight were really happy," McCann recalls. "Others, at Bellizzi, were saying things like, 'You don't want to get a check for performance.'"

McCann is not the kind of school leader who would set out to overtly elevate the Dwight teaching staff and goad the Bellizzi staff, but neither did she seek to avoid the spectacle. Part of what has made Dwight successful, after all, is a kind of better-than-the-rest ethos, the sort of corps elitism that rallies sports teams, the Marines, medical interns, and college students in demanding academic majors. And this is something McCann has encouraged and bred. "If you are in a culture of high performance, people will change their performance [just] being around people who wouldn't accept less," insists McCann. "No one in our community respects a slacker. It is a Type-A personality, a team approach. It is 'If you are on this team and you are not pulling your weight, you might not want to stay here.'"

Everybody Counts

It is not clear if McCann's approach to raising expectations and performance at Bellizzi was effective, since, according to Kishimoto, the very recent reopening of the Dwight-Bellizzi Asian Studies Academy saw many of the Bellizzi teachers moved or replaced and since McCann had the freedom to hire even from outside the district. McCann's leadership approach at Dwight, however, is worth considering. How can what she built there be extended to the larger turnaround school? During the 2008–2009 school year, for example, Dwight students reaching the "goal" level in the state tests (one level above "proficient") increased by 14 percent, landing the school on one of ConnCAN's "top ten in the state" school performance lists. This was especially impressive because the school received a nearly constant influx of new students, many of whom spoke little or no English. It is true that, like some immigrant populations, Dwight families are described as ambitious and goal oriented. This is often noted dismissively, as if such achievement is somehow less impressive. Yet it takes tremendous effort to help students learn English quickly enough to outperform city peers on state tests.

As principal, McCann constructed a strong culture in which teachers wanted to be good and were proud of being part of a high-performing school. There was also solid undergirding: teachers got training, support, and coaching about literacy for English language learners. Teachers know what to do.

What McCann does especially well is leverage human capital all around a child—teachers, staff, parents—to amplify learning. By having teachers and paraprofessionals collaborate at Dwight, she achieved a kind of multiplier effect. So when the paraprofessionals in the building received their bonus checks, it was more than a kindly nod. McCann used them as teachers and tutors to reinforce learning in small groups, effectively more than doubling her teaching staff. "Everybody counts," said McCann, as we strolled into a small, overheated classroom in which an AmeriCorps tutor was working with six third graders who were reviewing a math concept they learned in their regular classroom minutes earlier.

And even though many parents do not speak English and are new to this country, McCann helped orient them to American culture, including instilling the expectation that parents speak to teachers and are involved in their child's school. In nice weather she regularly set up a table in front of the school and served coffee—and conversation—to parents dropping off children. At Thanksgiving, the school gave each family a turkey. The school also held family math nights and parent literacy workshops to guide parents in reading to their children, even taking them on a field trip to the library to learn how to check out books. McCann and her staff also helped parents figure out precisely what reading level children were using the Developmental Reading Assessment (DRA) and lending them books at that level so children could practice successfully at home. "We say, 'You are the first teachers,'" observed McCann. "Every parent wants their child to be successful. I don't care what the situation is, whether you are educated or not. We start there."

Teachers at Dwight were expected to work hard. There was an understanding of what a Dwight teacher looked like. It meant your door was open to your colleagues, that you were part of grade-level data teams, that you took on committee work which supported the school accountability plan. According to McCann, "You have to be a formal or informal leader here. You can't just close your door and do your thing." Dwight teachers also came to school early. While contractually they needed to arrive by 8:05 A.M. for the start of school at 8:15, "I have staff here at 6:45," said McCann. "They may work harder than other teachers, but they can see firsthand that they are on the cutting edge."

The work hard culture has been balanced by teamwork, camaraderie, and rewards McCann arranged for the staff. While seeing children progress is great payback in itself, McCann recognized that gift cards to Dunkin' Donuts and school or office supply stores are small but pointed recognitions. She also arranged twice-monthly happy hours at nearby local restaurants (a round of cocktails on the administration). And she held a yearly professional development retreat at a nearby resort-style facility on the Connecticut shore. "It's really classy. It costs me $8,000 to $10,000, but that's a reward," she says. She had dressdown Fridays when teachers could wear jeans and college gear in what was meant as yet another reminder (in case kids miss the signals elsewhere) that higher education is the goal.

And for McCann there is a high effort–high reward aspect to her leadership that staff can plainly see. For school-level leaders pressing on their teachers and staffs to collaborate better, work harder, and achieve more, a principal's modeling matters. "I don't come in early, but I stay late," says McCann. "I am in their classrooms. I model. I teach. I don't just ask, ask, ask of you. I give, give, give of me."

5

TEACHERS—THE VERY FRONT
LINE OF REFORM

IT IS AN ENCOURAGING SIGHT. Two days before winter break in Ms. Tran's geometry class at Hartford Public High School's Law and Government Academy, only one of seventeen students has his head down and is sleeping through the lesson. And, to judge from the other students' responses, he's missing something fun.

Second-year teacher Linda Tran's very high heels click as she moves among desks passing out an assignment that looks more like free-form art than the math puzzler that it is. "Be creative. Do it however you want. There is no right or wrong answer," she says as she hands students sheets on which they are to design a patterned quilt using specified restrictions and criteria.

The students actually bend over their papers and get to work. Tran strolls around the room offering encouragement. "Just so you know, I see a lot of people taking the design on the paper and making it their own. Tish, can you hold up yours because that is really nice?"

Tran, who mouths her age to me and signals with her fingers *24* so students don't catch on ("I try to keep it a secret," she says), graduated from the University of Connecticut in 2008 with bachelor's and master's degrees and is now enrolled in another master's program with plans to pursue a doctorate in curriculum and administration. She says teaching feels a lot like she imagines parenting is and says that with some of her classes "it is what you would call a lot of hand-holding."

While policy makers, district leaders, and even principals have their eyes glued to metrics, teachers like Tran live with the emotional and practical challenges of helping students turn around their academic lives. In 2009, only 35 percent of the school's students achieved the state standard in math (and zero percent of students with special needs). Tran, who also teaches a class made up of predominantly special needs and English language learners, feels the pressure to push students—but she doesn't want them to crash. "A lot of these students have a lot of holes mathematically," she says. "If you don't provide that foundation or support, that's when students check out. Some check out faster than others, but in any classroom you have to have that support to help them build confidence."

At the same time, Tran loves the adrenaline-charged environment of school turnaround. The start-up nature of the school means there are inevitable distractions, like how to enforce the school uniform dress code. "Teachers have different opinions on what a 'dress shoe' is," she says. "Some may accept Timberland boots; some may not." And in a turnaround there is the pressure to stay on pace with the curriculum even as new things are thrown into the mix. "I know a lot of staff members get frustrated with, I don't want to call them 'initiatives,' but sometimes it feels we are trying to do so many things at once, we don't do one thing well. You end up just grazing," she says. "We only have so much time to prove ourselves as an academy."

Good Teachers Are Game Changers

Teachers in turnaround schools are squarely in the spotlight. They are the ones everyone is counting on to help students make up for lost (and wasted) time, to take kids who may be grade levels behind and get them to meet state standards quickly. In the best turnaround schools this is not happening solo; making big leaps quickly (especially at the high school level) depends on effective teacher collaboration and group problem solving. But in addition to getting at what kids are missing, teachers working with students who are far behind also must consider the how of approaching learning gaps. Inside the classroom, in the moment of a lesson, Tran observes that she must be balanced, driving kids without letting them get so overwhelmed that they just quit.

Tran's observation is a reminder that although a school might radically change how it operates and teachers may reorient themselves to turnaround plans, we cannot expect students to suddenly snap into place. They need to acclimate to a new environment and expectations, even be coaxed into believing they can achieve at a level that may be dramatically different from what they are used to.

The ability to connect with students while getting them to approach their learning with greater purpose and intensity takes a lot of skill. It also requires having the right sort of school support for teachers. The central role of the teacher—not as solo practitioner but as the responsibility-taker for student learning—is a characteristic common to several of the best-performing charter schools. While charter schools have had mixed success across the board, there are exemplary charters that have helped urban students make impressive gains. And they have done it, they will tell you, by focusing on classroom teaching.

"Our belief is that the single best thing we can do is recruit, develop, recognize, and reward teachers," says Achievement First's Dacia Toll. Toll is not talking about "appreciating" staff with lunches and sweeping praise. Blanket kudos, applied in a democratic manner, miss the differentiation that is applied to socially valued professions: some teachers are truly, breathtakingly talented at their jobs. And others are not. Rather, she is articulating a strategy for rapid student improvement that focuses intensely on the details of teaching—and the teacher. This is a dual-growth model in which feedback for students and teachers is frequent and specific. Each is working to get better.

Toll's point, and research supports this, is that it matters *who* is standing in front of the class. While in 1966 sociologist James Coleman drew a critical link between socioeconomic status and school success, laying groundwork for theories of the power and reach of social capital, there is more to the story. Research shows that the quality and effectiveness of the teacher can have a *dramatic* impact on student achievement. A key 2006 Brookings Institution report, *Identifying Effective Teachers Using Performance on the Job*, by Robert Gordon, Thomas J. Kane, and Douglas O. Staiger, considers the distribution of teacher impacts on 150,000 math students in 9,400 Los Angeles classrooms from 2000 to 2003. They found that top teachers can effectively help minority students close the achievement gap at the rate of ten percentile points per year. As a result, the authors contend that "having a top quartile teacher rather than a bottom quartile teacher four years in a row would be enough to close the black-white test score gap." In contrast, they found that teachers in the bottom quartile, or inexperienced teachers (those in their first two years of teaching), lost an average of five percentile points per year relative to students with similar baseline scores and demographics. But also worth noting, and central to the study's findings, was that paper qualifications like teacher certification are *not* good predictors of teacher quality. Teacher quality matters so much, the authors argue, that districts must do more to track the value-added quality of a teacher's performance instead of effectively disengaging. "Once teachers are hired," they write, "school districts typically do very little additional screening. Tenure is awarded as a matter of course after two or three years of teaching."

If top-quality teaching matters so much, then it would stand to reason that getting those teachers working with high-need pupils makes sense. Yet other research makes it obvious why we have a continuing achievement gap: the most inexperienced teachers (who have fewer than three years in the classroom) end up in high-poverty urban schools. In fact, research suggests that students who could most benefit from high-quality teachers don't get them. Whether considering peer-reviewed research or information submitted by states in their Race to the Top applications, data show that teachers in high-poverty schools generally have less experience and are of a lower quality than teachers in wealthy districts where students already achieve at higher levels. Several studies show that teachers in poor districts come from less competitive colleges, fail certification exams at higher rates, and are less likely to be certified in the areas in which they teach (though as the first study observes, certification has its limitations). Yet other research, including a study by William L. Sanders and June C. Rivers looking at Tennessee's value-added system, found that "as teacher effectiveness increases, lower achieving students are the first to benefit." This suggests the urgency of getting the best teachers into turnaround schools.

The notion of allocating teachers to where they are most needed is, of course, a great research-based idea that is complicated by real life. In practice, inexperienced (and often idealistic) teachers congregate in high-need, high-poverty schools. With research suggesting that it takes three years to become a competent teacher, this leaves poor students with green practitioners and lower-quality instruction. And then to compound matters, one-third of new teachers quit in the first three years, and half quit within five. This means that students who most need the best teachers and steady relationships get less experienced teachers and high turnover.

Although it's clear what's *not* working, it's harder to come up with solutions, particularly about how to efficiently identify highly effective teachers. How do you know who is really good? Obviously, there is a growing call to link student learning to teachers, but what is the best way to do this? It seems only half-useful to judge teachers based on annual state tests (assuming all grade levels are tested in every state, which they are not), because by the time gaps are spotted, it's late in the school year or, worse, the summer after the year has ended. And who is to shake out the variables between student skill, student performance, and teacher approaches?

Clearly, linking student learning and teacher performance needs to happen at numerous intervals throughout the year and be based on a variety of well-defined skills that matter. Some things teachers teach matter more than others. At the Ramon Betances Elementary School in Hartford (closed at the end of the 2009–2010 school year), for example, acting principal Karen Gray tracked student progress by teacher in math and reading readiness (a Hartford weakness) so she could gauge learning well before state test time in the spring.

In first grade, for example, she charted a key early reading indicator to see which students recognized which sounds go with which letters. In September, just 26 percent of the students met the criteria (the indicator essentially shows who is *not struggling* in learning to read). Gray, however, also broke down results by teacher. Students in the three first-grade classrooms scored 24 percent, 41 percent, and 14 percent. The middle teacher with 41 percent, Kathryn McEachern, had looped with her students, notes Gray, perhaps partly accounting for a higher score: "In September she did not spend three weeks on rules and routines."

In December, when students were retested, the scores were 65 percent, 100 percent, and 59 percent, respectively. (Growth was 41 percentage points, 59 percentage points, and 45 percentage points, respectively.) Gray used the analysis to arrange meetings between teachers and a literacy coordinator. "It was no longer a grade-level issue; it was an individual issue," she says of the urgent need to get all teachers on track so kids would learn to read. While more of McEachern's students began in a better position—perhaps because of the looping and good use of time in September—Gray asserts that she is such an effective teacher that "she could have taken any kids and gotten up to 100 percent." But, according to Gray, "the 59 percent [result belongs to] the most veteran teacher in that grade"—echoing the results of the Brookings Institute study.

The Quality Evaluation Problem

The possibility that whether a first grader learns to read or not depends on which classroom teacher he or she is assigned is disturbing but instructive. It seems outrageous that poor students who need a strong teacher start off their school careers as failures because they lack good lessons. Yet, if we know that every single child in McEachern's class will learn to read in first grade, that is powerful information.

The question is this: How can we leverage that knowledge so that every teacher in the grade gets the same (or similar) results? One of the problems at Betances was that Gray was the only one who had numbers to suggest which teachers were her strongest. There is no central repository, no data site. While it might be cumbersome or even counterproductive to share such detailed information, without a clear measure of teacher effectiveness, principals and parents lean on good or bad buzz in judging potential teachers. In April, when principals in Hartford make staffing decisions for the following year, for example, they get on the phone with friends at other schools to get the scoop on which teachers are good and which ones aren't. "You do your homework, you call around. 'Tell me about Stacey, tell me the truth,'" explains Stacey McCann, principal at the Dwight-Bellizzi Asian Studies Academy. "You either get the good ones first or you take who's on the leftover list."

One of McCann's frustrations is that principals do a poor job of removing ineffective teachers, instead preferring to rewrite job descriptions rather than going through the process of giving multiple negative evaluations. "You let a teacher skate, and then you know you will close out the position and the teacher will be someone else's problem," says McCann. "If you have an instructional coach and they are not effective and you reassign them to the classroom, they will post out—when you really should have evaluated them out. We have to weed out those who are low-performing and groom teacher leaders. If we all did that as administrators, we wouldn't have this problem."

The lack of reliable information on teacher quality is not just a problem in Hartford. It is a central, troublesome characteristic of schools across the country. There is heated debate about the value and effectiveness of evaluations conducted by principals: How effective are *they* at judging the quality of teachers? And the current system that rewards teachers who earn advanced degrees with higher pay scales may not actually result in better teaching. The frustrating contradiction is this: While we can observe and study notable differences in effectiveness between teachers, as authors Steven G. Rivkin, Eric A. Hanushek, and John F. Kain conclude in their Texas-based study "Teachers, Schools and Academic Achievement," "little of the variation in teacher quality is explained by observable characteristics such as education or experience."

At present, the major source of judgments about teacher quality are teacher evaluations, which are spottily conducted and of questionable value. Evaluations of tenured teachers may be done once in five years in some districts. In Boston, Superintendent Carol R. Johnson has clashed with the teacher union over plans to overhaul twelve schools and require teachers in six of them to reapply for their jobs. Almost half of the city's teachers had not been evaluated in at least two years.

The failure to do evaluations, or do them regularly, suggests that they are a weak tool. In Hartford, for example, data show that despite dismal student achievement, teacher evaluations are stunningly positive, raising obvious doubts about their usefulness. According to evaluation data for the 2008–2009 school year, 55 percent of teachers received the highest rating of "accomplished," while 44 percent received the second-highest rating of "competent." Only 5 percent were rated "need improvement" and less than 1 percent as "unsatisfactory." And this is in a district where the majority of students do not read at grade level.

Can Teacher Unions Be Part of Turnaround?

There is a serious need to better evaluate, support, and develop teachers, especially in high-poverty schools where we know that teacher quality is a critical factor in the quest to close the achievement gap. But too often, union-district tensions become a drag on reform. In Hartford, Andrea Johnson, president of the Hartford Federation of Teachers, says a pervasive "us and them" attitude has strained relations. The turnaround environment—and pressure for better results fast—has school leaders blaming teachers, she says, feeding a "gotcha syndrome" that makes it hard for the union and the district to work together. "Trust me, we want to be there. We want to be at the table, we want to be part of the solution. We don't want to be part of the same old problem, problem, problem."

Yet, the failure to think fresh on both sides feeds debates that are a waste of time, resources, and public goodwill toward educators and reform. For example, in Hartford, because teachers are truly the front-line actors in school turnaround, one of the things that frustrates principals and district leaders most is a contract provision (not uncommon in teacher contracts) that lets senior teachers "bump" more junior teachers out of a position in the event of layoffs. With a tight economy, in 2009–2010 Hartford laid off about 300 of the district's 2,500 teachers. The district hired almost all of them back, but not before they had been reshuffled. Principals in turnaround schools who had hired teachers for specific posts had some bumped and replaced with senior teachers whose certification qualified them for the job. There was little attention given to whether the teacher was in synch with the school design plan or even really wanted to be there.

The bumping has been so disruptive to some turnaround schools, says school design administrator Christina Kishimoto, that the district appealed to the state to issue a corrective action order that would overrule the bumping provision in the contract during times of layoffs. The state board of education in April 2010 ordered school administrators and union officials to meet and try to resolve their differences. Kishimoto, who says that the district wants to change it from a districtwide bumping to schoolwide seniority system so that marginally qualified teachers from one area of the system are not suddenly plunked down as key teachers in a turnaround school, is not hopeful. In the past, she says, "we have tried to open that conversation. The union won't even talk about it."

Tension between the teacher union and the school district in Hartford only makes turnaround more challenging. To a certain extent, the gulf represents contrasting visions about who teachers are and what their role is in reform. Where contracts "protect" teachers from having to attend too many staff meetings or to suffer through lunch duty (though some do specify that teachers must collect milk and lunch money), district leaders and entrepreneurial principals envision teachers as frontline reformers.

Hartford superintendent Steven Adamowski argues—that unions "will have to change." Unions, he says, "are trying to do the same things they were doing five years ago" when so much else in the education landscape has shifted. Not only are they out of synch with reform, he says, but also this younger generation of teachers is less interested in union representation. Most, though not all, charter schools have avoided unions, which leaders view as impeding their vision and authority. It's unlikely that teacher unions will vanish. Nor should they. But there are signs that unions may be willing to rethink their role, particularly in low-performing districts.

While Hartford's teacher contract looks fairly traditional, some unions are reshaping their work agreements. In October 2009, in an overwhelming 21–1 vote, the New Haven teacher union adopted a new contract with reform-friendly provisions that let the city close the worst-performing schools and bring in new management. Principals in designated "turnaround schools" can hire their own teachers. While teachers would be union members, they would commit to the school for two years and—this is key—be subject to working conditions attached to that school. "They shall be exempt from many School Board regulations and District policies and shall likewise be exempt from many provisions of the Collective Bargaining Agreement," the contract reads.

These words make education leaders like Scott Given of UP Schools and Dacia Toll of Achievement First perk up and listen—and consider signing on to turn around an in-district urban school with union teachers. "This is a huge deal," says Given, who plans to launch the organization's first district turnaround school in fall 2011 in Boston. When we spoke in spring 2010, he was seriously considering New Haven as a launch site and may yet partner will Toll to turnaround a school there. "The whole reason it is an appealing possibility is the collective bargaining agreement," he said. "As an organization, we strongly believe that in order to have a successful turnaround school you need full autonomy around human capital." The leader must be able to select the people in the building, remove those that do not mesh with the agenda, choose the curriculum, determine length of school day, devise a behavior management system, and formulate an evaluation system. Toll, who has discussed partnering with Given to do turnaround in New Haven, says picking teachers and assigning the terms of work is essential to getting charter school leaders to take over existing low-performing public schools—something education secretary Arne Duncan is eager to see happen.

Charter Schools: Teacher Development Is Core Business

One reason why high-performing charter school leaders and education organizations have been reluctant to enter traditional district schools is that the teaching culture is already set. Charter schools that have dramatically raised student achievement in high-poverty areas have done it, in part, by paying a lot of attention to the recruitment, hiring, and development of their teachers. They have also done it largely outside of unions, which has fed creation of a fresh, mission-based culture but has also, particularly in the early years of charter schools, fueled burnout among young teachers who found themselves overwhelmed by student needs and working almost endless hours (fielding and making calls and sending e-mails into the night and on weekends). As top-performing charters have evolved, some have made adjustments. Overwork is simply not sustainable.

The mission-driven vibe at high-performing urban charters has appealed to young college grads. This is one reason why, according to federal data, charter school teachers tend to be populated by young people while districts schools tend to have older teachers. For example, nearly one-third of charter school teachers are under thirty, as compared to

17 percent of district school leaders, according to the 2007–2008 U.S. Department of Education Schools and Staffing Survey. (The gap in average age is more modest: 37.9 years for charter teachers and 42.3 years for district school teachers.)

Because so many charter school teachers are young and may have never worked in education before, or have relatively little experience, teacher induction, development, and mentoring are, *by necessity*, core work at charter school organizations. The top-performing charters take this seriously. They need strong systems to bring along teachers at the same time that they are serving a high-need urban population. In the best instances, doing this work out in the open and constantly can feed a dynamic environment in which teacher-centered evaluation, discussion, and improvement is in the air. It can also bring some order to the work of turnaround by taking what can feel like a hurricane of initiatives and focusing student improvement and experience through teacher development. You prioritize your mission by what you ask teachers to do and how you judge their performance.

Inexperience has drawbacks, but strong charter schools have systems in place so that a new teacher gets support as part of the natural cycle of the school's work. At Achievement First, for example, teachers meet weekly with their mentor, or coach, and every six weeks schools have Data Day. While students have a day off, teachers gather in teams to analyze student assessment data and plan instruction. And instead of a traditional evaluation, each Achievement First teacher has a "Professional Growth Plan." These documents (similar to those for school leaders) assume that everyone is in the midst of improving, is eager for advice, and is tackling trouble spots. This turns evaluation from a *gotcha!* exercise into a process of discussion and goal setting. Teachers assess themselves and are assessed by a mentor in seven broad areas: student achievement and character development, core instructional excellence, classroom culture, planning and data analysis, student and family relationships, personal organization and effectiveness, and core values and responsibilities.

Achievement First's internal documents show that teachers are assessed on, for example, how well they let "students understand unambiguously that the teacher cares about them and their progress." They are expected to have "positive framing" when correcting student behavior. Teachers must "consistently use rigorous, bite-sized, measurable, standards-based aims to drive instruction" and build opportunities into each lesson for "independent practice so that students have ample, successful 'at bats' to practice." It is the teacher's job to motivate students so that "100% of students are on task and at least 80% of hands are in the air." Teachers must model key values. "Is humble, honest, and admits mistakes," reads one checklist item.

This is not to say that districts and individual schools don't have effective professional development or mentoring programs. Rather, the point is the *structure* of how a charter organization like Achievement First takes practices and explicitly articulates these and then assesses teachers on how they meet them. In effect, by giving it a check box on the assessment/personal growth plan, they are setting some clear and well-defined expectations.

Not every teacher, however, wants to be judged on how much "joy" they pack into their lessons. Charter schools certainly are not for everyone. That is why Achievement First, like KIPP and other top charter schools, invests substantial time and energy in recruiting a certain type of teacher. Achievement First has a full-time recruiting team with one recruiter for every thirty staff positions they fill. Recruiters build a pool of candidates and conduct initial screenings before a teacher candidate ever sits down with a principal. The aim, says Toll, is "to take as much as possible off the plate of the principal."

Those that pass the first round of screening return to the school to conduct an on-site teaching demonstration and get feedback. "The feedback is an important part of the interview process," says Toll, noting that how a candidate reacts to comments and criticism is a big piece of deciding who to hire. Content knowledge is important, especially in middle and high school, but more critical is being able to *explain* the content and be open to reworking lessons, what Toll calls "a continuous improvement mind-set." While the image of the high-performing charter school teacher may be someone who is brainy and exuberant but inexperienced in classroom techniques, that is changing at top schools like Achievement First. When hiring, Toll says, they look for people with a passion for pedagogy. Yes, they need to know content, she says, "but they have to be geeky about it, an 'instructional geek,' someone interested in the nuances of instruction. Those are our best teachers." Then there is how a candidate projects himself or herself. "They have to love kids. There has to be some level of personal warmth that is going to be clear to one of our scholars" (Achievement First students are called "scholars").

Despite the strong screening, however, every teacher doesn't work out. Achievement First "non-renews" contracts of 4–5 percent of teachers each year. "If someone is really struggling, we know it soon so it is not a surprise," says Toll. Because new teachers receive "lots and lots of feedback," she says there is typically rapid growth. When that doesn't happen and supports don't work, it becomes clear they don't belong in the classroom. In addition, some teachers leave, most often because they move or go to graduate school, giving Achievement First a 17–19 percent turnover rate each year.

This is not necessarily a bad thing, given that ineffective teachers who hang on in a school really do hurt student learning. What's encouraging now is that so many people want to teach. Scott Given said that when he led the turnaround of Excel Academy in East Boston, as principal he received about 2,500 resumes per year for a handful of spots. "There is no question in my mind that there is a large cohort of people who are willing to work very hard."

Hiring Teachers Who Share the Vision

Achievement First, like the top-performing charter schools, has benefited from creating powerful school cultures and by hiring teachers who buy into the mission. This approach does not have to be owned by charter schools. Some turnaround principals are seizing on the mission-based energy to unite faculty around some serious achievement challenges. Terrell Hill, principal of Hartford's High School, Inc., did not have broad power to set working conditions (his school day, for example, is determined by the bus schedule), but in hiring he sought out teachers who would be dedicated to his vision and have a do-what-it-takes attitude. "I am looking for committed employees, not contract employees," he says. "I want people who I believe will be loyal to me and not to the contract."

As someone who walks around the school picking up papers and who gets out a paint brush and roller himself (even enlisting his daughters to help), Hill values teachers who showed up in the summer before opening to help get the school ready. To find his teachers, Hill had a straightforward, visceral-reaction approach in screening those candidates he would interview. "I went to schools around the district. I would go into classrooms unannounced. If I liked what I saw, I waited until the end of class and I introduced myself. If I didn't, I just walked away."

Hill is quick to complain that he got "stuck" with a few teachers he didn't want to hire, but, overall, he is happy with his staff. It is too early to know how well he did, how well they will all work together, or how well they will do in helping students at the school actually perform academically. But on one afternoon in room 402, a pregnant and pony-tailed Heidi Bothamly is teaching algebra I to a class of students who actually seem interested in learning the material. The problem on the SMART Board: $3x + 4 = 10$.

"Okay, Tiffany, can you explain how you got 1?" asks Bothamly. Tiffany, a girl with confident body language and hair pulled tight and coiled on top of her head, slips out of her desk seat, grabs a marker from the front of the room, and quickly—too hurriedly for Bothamly's liking—works through the problem. "Tiffany, can you take a second and go through your written work?" asks Bothamly.

Hill, standing near the door sipping from a water bottle (which he drains and taps on his thigh), adds encouragement. "C'mom, girl, break it down." Tiffany does, explaining why $x = 2$.

"How could Tiffany check her work?" Bothamly asks the class.

What's noteworthy about this class is not the academics. The problem (and the ones that followed) is sadly simple for ninth-grade algebra. In a typical suburban school, this work would be included in a seventh-grade pre-algebra course. The reality of urban teaching is that kids are behind. What feels hopeful here is that every student is comparing his or her own work with what's on the board, and, perhaps most striking, when a kid wearing glasses suddenly sneezes, a chorus of *Bless you!* rises from students still hunched over their papers. He sneezes again. *Bless you!* There is a politeness and civility present here that is too often painfully absent in many urban schools. It is easier to do your work when you are not worried about being whacked, shoved, or dissed.

"Man, if I could just clone her," Hill says afterward in the hallway. "How does an earthy, crunchy white girl keep the wildest kids focused?"

Hill wants his teachers to do more than they are supposed to do, but he is also willing to bend for them. When a teacher heading the student council wanted to take kids down the street to collect end-of-day baked goods from Au Bon Pain, package the goods individually, and deliver them to a church soup kitchen down the street as a community service, Hill knew that officially organizing a field trip and getting approvals would complicate and stall the effort. Instead, he told her to just sign out and go (now they do it as a regular service). And when he was warned that the sixty-three-year-old Vietnam vet and high school chemistry teacher he wanted to hire would be trouble, he ignored naysayers. "People said, 'He'll fight you every step of the way,'" recalls Hill. But when Mark Oakman, whose longish white hair curls up at the back of his neck, quietly conferences with a student while others tap away on netbooks, room 410 is the picture of chem lab write-ups in progress. Hill likes Oakman, whom he refers to as a "gruff old soldier dude." The fact that Oakman is the union representative in the building is just fine with Hill. "He doesn't want to be the union rep protecting weak people," observes Hill, who himself served three years' active duty in the U.S. Army, stationed in Frankfurt leading up to the fall of the Berlin Wall in 1989.

For his part, Oakman says he's more than happy to have his performance judged on how well his students do on state tests. "Rate me with these kids," he says. "These are my kids. These kids, when they take the CAPT [Connecticut Academic Performance Test], I want credit for it. I don't want any of this long-term you think you are owed something. I say, go get 100 kids, loop with them, have them take that test—and see how we do."

Oakman's style clearly jibes with Hill's approach. "Terrell brings a standard of conduct that he will not allow to sag and he will not allow to be changed. This is what you strive for. And if you don't get there, it doesn't mean you are a failure, it doesn't mean you are below average; it means you have work to do to get to that standard." Oakman, who served in a combat unit on the ground in Vietnam from April 1969 to April 1970, approaches his teaching challenge like a soldier. "I have always had a boss. When the boss lays out the mission, you look at your assets and your non-assets, you look at your problems and you put together a plan," he says, noting that the mission here is not in terms of weeks but is a four-year press to get freshmen utterly turned around, prepared, and reoriented by graduation.

Despite embracing what feels like a boot camp philosophy of success, Oakman's personal story includes challenges that make his presence at High School, Inc. surprisingly relevant to his students. As a youth, he flunked out of Southern Connecticut State College (now University) but managed to reengage in school and earn two master's degrees from Duke University. He carved a career in the chemical industry and eight years ago returned to teaching (he taught in North Carolina early in his career). "I wasn't a high flyer in education," he says. "I know what it means to be given a second chance. I also know what it means to be totally in fear of not being around the next day. I know what it takes to get an education, and I know what it takes to survive."

Urban Teaching Takes More

Jocelynne Jason came to Taft High School in Cincinnati (now renamed Taft Information Technology High School) in the late 1990s to teach eleventh- and twelfth-grade English. "It was a nuthouse," she recalls. "There was no concern about grades. I never had a student ask me about their grades. And there might be three people in a class that was supposed to have twenty-seven, and two would be asleep. It was crazy. I really thought, 'What the devil have you gotten yourself into. Why did you come here?'"

Jason, who has taught now for thirty-three years, came to Taft from the suburbs and says that those who think you can hone your classroom skills in urban schools and then go teach in the suburbs do not fully appreciate the differences in what is required of teachers in the two settings. This idea—understanding the cultural context of the school in which you are teaching—has become a powerful and important force shaping the education of urban teachers.

This is the philosophy behind urban teacher residency programs in which teachers intern like medical residents in the city schools in which they will be placed to acclimate them and help them understand aspects of teaching specific to that school. The goal is better-quality teachers in poor city schools—and teachers who don't quit in year one or two because they are blindsided by challenges that are not part of most teacher training programs. This approach has, for example, allowed the Boston Teacher Residency program to report an 86 percent retention rate among its graduates six years out and Chicago's Academy for Urban School Leadership to have 83 percent of its teachers still teaching in city schools five years out. Compare that with the 40–50 percent of new teachers who quit teaching within the first five years.

Jason says that coming to Taft has made her a better teacher, even though it meant starting from scratch. "I couldn't depend on tried-and-true methods that had worked in the suburbs," she says. Academically, "everything had to be broken down more." Although she could see that students had intelligence, they lacked the skills that come from practice and experience. They could not take something as basic as a writing prompt and formulate a written response. "You couldn't take anything for granted. You couldn't assume any prior knowledge."

Part of the problem, according to Jason, is that before school turnaround at Taft there was a huge disconnect between student academic work and grades. "I remember a student coming to me saying, 'I got an A in math.' I said to him, 'Well, that's great!' He said, 'No, it's not. I don't know any math.'" The problem of grades, especially in high-poverty urban schools, is a serious one. It is not uncommon today to see schools where average student GPAs are surprisingly high and high numbers of students (relatively speaking) enrolled in Advanced Placement courses and yet where SAT scores are low and *none* of the students who take the College Board AP tests score high enough to earn credit. Even in schools that look like successes, there are teachers who look askance at those who earn diplomas, wondering if they really earned them.

Passing state tests, after all, is only part of the requirement. Students must also pass their high school courses, which in recent years have become more numerous as graduation requirements have increased across the country. Teachers want to help kids, but they grow frustrated, as one teacher observed, "when they are not held to any standards" and assigned better grades than they earn or are passed when they have not actually passed. "You have a kid who fails every class in ninth grade but then that kid the next year is taking tenth-grade classes," says one teacher. "What message does it send to the kids who actually try?"

At Taft, Jason says turnaround has made a difference not just in student achievement but also in how they work in her classroom. When we spoke in the spring of 2010, it had been eight years since Anthony Smith became principal and several years since students began consistently passing all state graduation tests at extremely high percentages. Jason says there are still difficult days teaching, but far fewer of them. In the past, she says, "I felt like a steel ball in a pinball machine, and every time the bell rang, it was like someone was pulling back the spring and letting it go."

The school is still pushing to get students to work harder, to do more. For example, a capstone project that is just getting off the ground is not pulled together and feels like it could flop. But turnaround and working in this environment, she says, has pushed her to be better. "In any building, there are motorboats, there are barges, and there are rocks," she says, noting that she heard this analogy made by someone else and has latched onto it. "I have become a motorboat. I always had that, but I have been given the opportunity to present new ideas." Jason says she notices that students rise to more serious demands. "My kids respond best when their time is not wasted. They want to be successful."

In March 2010, after I had interviewed Jason, we corresponded by e-mail. I asked Jason what made her students come in, sit down, focus, and care about doing well. She decided to ask her seniors and e-mailed back their responses. Their list:

- the desire to succeed
- it's our routine
- that's what school's for
- the challenge
- good classroom management
- organization
- everything is connected
- you're a mean bitch, but in a good way—tough love (LMAO!)
- no spoon-feeding
- repetition of procedures
- seniors are mature
- structure
- something productive happens every day
- demand/command respect
- comfortable with each other
- trust each other to work together
- we have a goal in mind—college

- we just follow the pattern
- want to graduate
- you need some knowledge in your brain
- understanding and accepting the importance of education.

"So that's what they say," she wrote. Then she added a list of her own:

- I never want to waste my students' time. I am embarrassed to not be prepared.
- I have the support of my principal.
- I work hard and provide a good example of work ethic.
- I'm in charge of my classroom—sort of a benevolent dictator.
- I focus on missing skills—if they aren't doing an assignment or are doing it poorly, I don't assume it's by choice; I mean really, who wakes up in the morning and says, "I'm going to do the worst job I can today"? I figure out what skills seem to be missing, present those skills for practice with "recipes" (step-by-step procedures) to follow and we try again.
- I use relevant materials; if a reading does not *seem* to be relevant, we *find* the relevance.

"That's about all I can figure out," she wrote in closing. That's quite a lot.

New Rules, New Relationships

When Cheryle Kelleher, who teaches tenth-grade biology at Taft Information Technology High School, agreed to follow principal Anthony Smith from the middle school where she was teacher and where he was principal to one of the district's worst city high schools, she paused. "I was going to a school with a horrible reputation. There were shootings near the school. You would hear stories of fights." For this mother of three children who lives in the suburbs and whose children attend private schools (her oldest is in college), Taft was a different world.

And then there was the fact that she and three other teachers were coming with Smith to a school in which the rest of the faculty had been there, in some cases, for decades. When Smith stood up before the staff and introduced them as his "dream team," she recalls, "I just wanted to hide under the table." Teachers can be as back-biting as the kids they teach. Kelleher recalls a cool reception. "It is the look, the glare, the non-speaking in the hallways," she says. "I was very nervous coming in here." Since then, any tensions have given way to collegial relationships. Kelleher says she admires her peers, including Jason. "Jocelynne is a great teacher. She does not put up with anything. She has a reputation of being one of those teachers you want to have."

Kelleher credits Smith for making the school a safe environment for teachers and students. Having a principal who enforces rules changes how students behave, she says. "I would not be telling you the truth if I said I never heard a profane word in the hallways." (To be fair, she notes, even in her oldest son's parochial school "they were dropping F-bombs.") But "I can say without hesitation that [Smith] has your back. When he has your back and students know that, you have fewer problems." Kelleher now brings her children to Taft for basketball games and school events. Instead of feeling nervous, her family is "proud that I teach here. You see the impact you have on these kids' lives. It makes teaching worthwhile when you know you are doing a good job."

The power of teachers to change students' lives is an underestimated force in school turnaround. Just as focus is on systems and revamped curriculum and methods for reaching scores—and certainly that is important—it is also clear that children in high-poverty schools need connections with grownups who care about what's happening in their world. They may look inattentive in class, but students say teachers are powerful influences. And despite the presumption that students don't want to apply themselves, working hard actually makes them feel relevant and valued.

Shaquana Cochran, an eighteen-year-old senior enrolled in the Nursing Academy at Hartford Public High School, actually *likes* best the teacher who demands more because, as Jason's list hints, it represents a form of respect. Cochran, in fact, cannot stop talking about her English teacher during a group conversation with seven other students. "She gives us *two hours'* worth of homework a night, and I'm not even lyin'," Cohran says in a boastful tone. "I have another teacher who says, 'I hope you read the pages.' The other teacher, she makes it fun. She tries to put the stereotypes in the dirt, like that Hartford has bad kids."

Kids want to do well, says Joan Massey, assistant superintendent for secondary schools in Hartford. "My philosophy is that if kids are walking in the door, they want something. I don't believe kids come to school as a social venture, because they have other opportunities for that. They really want to get an education. They know their life will be better if they are reading at an adult level."

Teaching in Hartford right now, says Massey, is not easy. But there is benefit in the fact that so many teachers are wrestling with the same changes and having the same conversations. Collaboration is a central part of revamping a school, because there is simply too much to do and figure out for each teacher to tackle alone. "Creating a positive environment with adults is key. We're focusing on effective teaching. We're focusing on data teams. We are talking about strategies, transparency, and evidence," she says. "We are talking more about student work, student achievement, how to help students move forward."

Students like Carlanna Dyer, a senior at the Law and Government Academy at Hartford Public High School, may or may not perceive a difference in the behind-the-scenes work her teachers do and the richer collaborative relationships they are building. But her school day experience is starting to change. Dyer says she was all into her friends and slacking off until she recently connected with one of her teachers. "I know that's clichéd," she says. "But I have a close relationship with my teacher, and she pushes me every time I get to this point where I think I can't do it."

Burnout and Recharge

Urban school turnaround is a high-energy proposition. Time is short, and there are days in which the work seems endless and results out of reach. Near the end of one school day just before winter break, Bridget Allison, the lawyer-turned social studies teacher who led the design team that created the Law and Government Academy at Hartford Public High School, sinks into the chair behind her desk and crosses her legs. She is wearing a bright-red sweater, corduroy pants, and stylish square glasses framed by super-straight, dark reddish-brown hair. She is the picture of smart, edgy, urbane. And she is depleted.

"I am exhausted," she says. "I am almost there [at the breaking point]. Every year the well runs dry and I have a summer, but it never goes up to the level of where it was before. Next year I just cannot maintain the pace that I am maintaining this year. Thank God I don't have any children of my own."

The problem is that in smaller, leaner schools there are fewer people to do things that need to be done. In addition to teaching three classes of social studies and serving as dean of students, Allison is also in charge of leading 105 seniors, guiding them as they prepare for graduation and what comes after. She is evaluating their transcripts to figure out if they are missing courses and, with the help of the sole guidance counselor in the school, must create students' course schedules. By hand.

The teaching itself is also wearing. Her subject may be social studies, but Allison says that, if she really gets right down to it, content teachers like her are teaching reading and writing, skills students never learned. "I recognize that that is the nature of the beast," she says, "but I spend a lot of time on 'this is how you take notes, this is how you break down a paragraph.' And I teach seniors. What I am concerned about is, 'Can I get these kids to be successful in college?'" And when Allison is talking about college, she is not talking about the most competitive institutions. She is talking about any form of higher education. Will students be able to read and write sufficiently well to even have a toe-hold?

In the middle of the interview, something interrupts Allison's I'm-spent monologue. It is a visit from a fit young man wearing faded jeans, tan Timberland work boots, and a "Hartford Public football" T-shirt. He strides into her classroom and flashes the self-confident and expectant grin of a former student returning to visit a former teacher in the days leading up to Christmas. He says he has one more semester at Southern Connecticut State University before getting his degree but that he's continuing on to get his doctorate in educational leadership. "It's a five-and-a-half-year program," he explains.

He catches Allison's tired words and body language and counters them. "You can't stop, you got to keep it going," he says. Keep it going for all the kids like him in the poor neighborhoods. "You come from a single-parent family from Hartford," he says. "I can talk to my boys the way I want to—but I can also go to a white-tie affair and talk to people." He wants kids from Hartford to know that they *can belong* in college, that it's not just for other people. Like him, they need help getting past doubting themselves. "If you ever want me to come in to your class and talk, I'd love to," he offers, and then he opens his arms. "One more hug?"

He stands, radiant. She is on her feet. She says she's going to cry.

"I just wanted to say thank you," he says. "You helped me a lot."

When he leaves, she says that teaching is like a crack addiction. "I'm exhausted right now, but I love my job."

6

PARTNER FOR HELP AND CHANGE

THE PUSH TO RAISE TEST SCORES and help kids in failing urban schools achieve academically is important. It is increasingly clear, however, that educational equity is not merely about book learning but also about teaching students the skills they need to access networks critical to life success. A growing number of education leaders, particularly those in turnaround schools, are talking about social capital, which, they realize, is important to help students develop people skills and savvy, to learn how to make connections, and to understand how the professional world operates. Alongside such skills, students also need a vision of what their future could look like—take Adam Johnson's hunger to have his students "see Hartford from the twenty-sixth floor"—and the confidence to try new things. Turnaround is about raising test scores, yes. But it is also about changing lives.

As a result, helping poor urban kids get social polish and firsthand career experience is becoming a centerpiece of turnaround work. The goal is to overcome the thin networks that often limit poor students. For example, research shows that students in high-poverty neighborhoods may have strong family and friendship networks, but they lack relationships with people outside of their community who can connect them to new opportunities. A 1998 study by Xavier de Souza Briggs, on a leave from MIT to direct the Obama administration's Office of Management and

Budget, followed 132 low-income African American and Latino teens and found that more than one-quarter could not think of a single adult in their lives outside of their households who would be a good source of job information. And a 2003 study of class-based differences in parent networks found that while middle-class families built connections based on their children's activities, poor families' connections were rooted in kinship ties. Erin McNamara Horvat, Elliot B. Weininger, and Annette Lareau, authors of *From Social Ties to Social Capital: Class Differences in the Relations Between Schools and Parent Networks*, observed that "middle class families, largely as a result of their network ties, have considerably greater resources at their disposal."

Increasingly, however, schools are using *their* networks to create social capital building experiences for their students. In fact, the very notion of schools forging partnerships with nonprofits, educational institutions (colleges and universities), and corporations and local businesses has become a critical piece of the reform engine, both as direct benefit to students in raising social capital and, more broadly, for schools in supporting reform and more hands-on learning. In a 2010 report on partnerships from the Center for School Change at Macalester College, Jasmine Blanks, Naima Bashir, and Joe Nathan argue that it's just common sense for schools to partner as a way to increase effectiveness and efficiency. The report outlines "essential factors" in collaborations that include identifying clear and important needs, being willing to experiment with new ideas, recognizing mutual goals, starting small, being honest with partners about strengths and weaknesses, investing resources to make the partnership work, and assessing how it's going.

The report also points out that collaborations "are not a quick fix" for narrow problems but are designed to find "efficient strategies in turbulent, competitive situations." It is tempting for schools to partner with whoever offers help, but schools must be somewhat picky. Partnerships need to be meaningful and fruitful, because schools cannot afford to spend so much energy and time just for the sake of having a partner. How useful is a partnership that doesn't really benefit students?

Finding the Right Partner

In Cincinnati, Taft Information Technology High School principal Anthony G. Smith says he inherited an ineffective tutoring program funded by a major corporation that vaguely aimed "to motivate kids to do the right thing." He says there were multiple problems with the program, including when tutoring was scheduled (after school, so kids didn't show up), and there was little focus or accountability around the tutors' skills or what they were covering. "They were supposed to cover the whole gamut," says Smith. "However, they were just there. They really didn't offer anything." Smith went to meet with the group, and after deciding they weren't adding anything productive to his school, he says, "I asked for them never to come back."

Today the school has a very powerful partnership with Cincinnati Bell, a communications and entertainment company with 3,000 employees. And while one part of that relationship does include tutoring students, Smith says it is run very differently from the old program. Now they look at data to figure out what areas students need help mastering to pass state tests, and then they match that need with tutors' skills. Before "we just thought the adults were smarter than the kids." Tutoring now happens on Wednesdays and Thursdays from 9 to 10 A.M., and company vans transport fifty Cincinnati Bell employees from three different sites to and from Taft, says Carolyn Martinez, Bell's communication director who manages the tutoring program, which serves sixty to seventy students at a time.

Martinez says they receive information from Taft about what specific sections of the five-part state test students are struggling with and match tutors according to their skills. She says they also give tutors prep books with explanations, sample tests with answers, useful Web sites, and tips on how to work with students. Taft also gives a training presentation outlining strategies. Tutors sit at the same seats in the school cafeteria in each session, so students can easily find them, Martinez says, and tutors are also reminded to stay on task for the hour.

"We tell the tutors in training, 'It is not about hearing about their problems—their mother, their sister, their bro in jail. You can be their friend to a point, but you are there to tutor them.'" That said, the tutors and students do form bonds. A few years ago Bell sales consultant Jeanna Jones tutored a student who was pregnant. When she went into labor, the student called Jones. "She knew that I would come," says Jones. "I represented stability in her life."

For employees, Martinez says the tutoring is a way to give back, and because it is supported by the company and precisely scheduled (the van doesn't wait for stragglers), employees can plan because they know exactly when they will be back in their office. Plus, says Martinez, "people know. It is acceptable, you are going to leave work and go tutor. It's not, 'Oh I'm too busy.'" It is so endorsed by the company, in fact, that Cincinnati Bell routinely highlights tutors within the company for special attention, giving them tickets to Cincinnati Reds baseball games, for example. At one May 2010 ball game, a Taft student was invited to throw out the first pitch—and a tutor was designated to catch it.

The relationship is so valuable, says Mike Turner, senior institute manager and program facilitator at Taft, that the school is extremely careful about how they communicate with the company. "Anthony [Smith] has designated people here who are the only people who make contact with Cincinnati Bell. We have a valuable partnership, and we want to preserve that partnership."

Why Partnerships Make Sense—on Both Sides

Cincinnati Bell CEO Jack Cassidy does have what he calls a "benevolent spirit," but he says the partnership with Taft Information Technology High School also makes economic sense. "At the end of the day, the shareholders don't care about my benevolent side. They care about profit and loss." His company's business success, he says, is tied to the quality of his employees and the quality of his customers. The best way to impact those two factors, he observes, is by improving schools and, in turn, job opportunities and earning prospects for students and the people in the community his company serves. In his case, as the leader of an information technology and communications company, he sees that there is a serious divide between people who have access to the Internet and technology and those who don't.

What's clear about the Taft-Bell partnership is that its effectiveness owes as much to *what* Bell has brought as to *how* the alliance has unfolded. And credit for this goes to Taft principal Anthony Smith and Cassidy. Smith says many school leaders "have trouble when it comes to business, especially big business. The first thing people ask them for is money. We never ask for money. We ask for resources." In fact, says Cassidy, the only time the company has actually invested a large dollar amount—$200,000–300,000, plus help from Bell business partners like Cisco, the telephone and computer integration company—was when the school first opened. The goal of that investment, says Cassidy, was to put more computing power in Taft than anywhere else in the district. "Frankly, that was the last time we gave the school any money," says Cassidy. "Of course, over the last eight or nine years we have done everything—hold the mother-of-all-tailgate parties to raise money for instruments for the band. We didn't give them money; we held the event and the kids had to work the event."

What Bell has offered is better than cash: connections and opportunity. It is more valuable to Taft to have Bell draw in other companies, organize fund-raising events, send in company employees to tutor—all activities that build deeper support and social capital for and among the school and students—than simply to provide dollars that are spent and gone.

One of the things that concerned Cassidy early on, however, was the perception that he and his company represented a white savior for a poor black community. He sought counsel from two friends who run a company called Global Lead, a diversity consulting firm to Fortune 1000 companies. They suggested Cassidy meet with West End community members, which he did, sitting down in a gathering space in the midst of housing projects. What Cassidy discovered by listening to their assessment of needs was that they were on the same page. "The things they suggested were things we wanted to happen," he says. And, in fact, community members were excited about students learning technology skills and asked if the students could in turn teach them what they learned. This spurred Bell to set up a computer lab and hold an evening program at Taft where students would teach West End residents how to use computers and the Internet. The lab was lost when Taft was transferred to temporary space, but Cassidy says they will restart the program in the new school building.

While Bell provides tremendous support to Taft, most of it relates to their core business, to things they already have or that they produce. Because Cassidy feels so strongly that students need access to the Internet, Bell's incentive program provides all technology program students who earn a GPA of 3.3 or higher with the use of a laptop and a cell phone. They have given out 280 laptops (thirty in the 2009–2010 school year) and have never taken one back for a fallen GPA. Bell also wires the students' homes for high-speed Internet access. ("Poor families can't afford broadband, but college exists on the Internet," says Cassidy.) And Bell offers paid summer internships for a handful of top Taft students and each year ten renewable $5,000 scholarships for seniors pursing information technology (IT) degrees in college.

Cincinnati Bell CEO Jack Cassidy: Here's My Cell Number

Cassidy believes that partnerships with schools and students must be personal. "The key variable is 'Go big or stay home,'" he says. "You are either all in or you are not, because these kids can smell bullshit from five miles away. Ninety-nine percent of adults these kids have met in their lives have disappointed them." In concrete terms, that means that Cassidy shows up at football games. He talks with the basketball team. He plans to teach a class in marketing. He shows up at the school unannounced. "I have to know what is going on at the ground level," he says. To be an effective partner to a school, "you don't have to recreate the world and you don't have to throw hundreds of millions of dollars. You have to not only show but exemplify your personal commitment to the school."

And that commitment means that the CEO has to have a relationship with the school principal or leader. He knows the superintendent, but his primary relationship is with Anthony Smith at Taft. And while there are a few people at Bell who help manage the partnership, he is the one who meets with Smith. Cassidy's personal investment sends a powerful message to Cincinnati Bell employees. For those who do tutoring, for example, this high-profile involvement provides a "connectivity to the mission," making employees happy the company supports something they care about and enjoy. While the tutoring is ostensibly about learning and preparing for state tests, it is most powerfully about relationships. "Kids will work harder for a tutor then they will work for themselves," says Cassidy. "When the kids are involved with a tutor, all of a sudden they are not in this game alone."

In case any kid at Taft *ever* does feel alone or in trouble, however, they have someone they can call: Cassidy gives every student at Taft his personal cell phone number. He tells the kids that if they are about to make a decision and they don't know what the right choice is, they'd better call him. Because, he says, "if you go ahead and make the wrong decision and say, 'There was no one I could talk to,' I say, 'That is bullshit because you had my number and you didn't run down your string of options.'"

Cassidy says he gets a call from a Taft student about once every six to seven weeks. One student called when his house burned down; a girl who plays for the basketball team called when she broke her arm and was having trouble getting medical care. And then there was the phone call several years ago from Taft's valedictorian two months before she was to go to Ohio State University. Cassidy recalls, "She said, 'You don't know this, but my father was shot to death in front of me and my brother and my sisters, and my mother is literally a crack whore and she is back on the pipe, and I can't stand all these men coming through our house. Can I come and live with you?'" Cassidy found her a place to live, though not with his family. But when kids dial up asking for free phone cards, he's clear. "I tell them they've got the wrong guy."

The partnership requires deep involvement, but Cassidy insists that he has been the winner. "I get a thousand times more out of this program than what I give." Says this man who never graduated from college, "I want to see these kids—my kids and the kids in the West End—achieve something I wasn't able to do. I see the economic benefit, not only to them, but to society."

Hartford: Making It Real (Is Not Always Easy)

One goal of partnerships is to offer students an entrée into a network they wouldn't typically be able to access. In Hartford, Superintendent Steven Adamowski has tried to design social capital into district reform work by insisting all schools have uniforms (high school uniforms foreshadow career dress) and that every turnaround school be paired with an outside organization. "Every one of our redesigned schools has an external partner," he says. In the case of industry, he says, "they can verify curriculum, if not be an angel to the school and help run it." The list of partners is long and impressive, from top law firms and the University of Connecticut Law School to Travelers Insurance to nonprofits like Our Piece of the Pie (OPP), a social service agency working with students at OPPortunity High School who are at risk of dropping out (and yes, helping run that school).

The uniforms, particularly in high school, reinforce to students that there is something that comes next, or, as Kerry Swistro, a veteran teacher at Bulkeley High School, offered during a school choice fair, "It's great for kids because it gives them a way to process why they are attending the schools they are attending." Although the khaki pants, white shirt, maroon tie, and blazer required of Bulkeley's eleventh- and twelfth-grade students (including those in the teacher prep program) may not be typical classroom educator wear, junior Renee Santiago likes the uniform: "We look nice. We look professional. We look like we're ready to work."

And they are working. Part of Bulkeley's teacher prep program that Santiago is enrolled in has her and classmate Rachel Jones spending time in a kindergarten classroom. "Right now we are working with puppets to teach children about different kids' ethnic backgrounds," she says, adding that many teachers in city schools are white. "We are diverse," adds Santiago. "I'm Puerto Rican. She [Jones] is black. It's important to have diverse teachers. I think we will be able to impact people's lives." The idea of early exposure to careers, particularly careers that capture students' interest, can be motivating. Swistro confirms that Jones, who had been especially shy, is "blossoming." And Jones says getting to work with children has her earning As and Bs in her teacher prep courses.

However, it is one thing to allow high school students to help out in familiar settings like a kindergarten classroom and quite another to send them to a law firm. While that may be the very point of forging such partnerships, it looks more complicated on the ground. Adam Johnson, principal at the Law and Government Academy at Hartford Public High School, knows that a huge percentage of his students arrive in tenth grade several grade levels behind in reading. And yet he is desperate for them to spend time in high-end firms. Law and Government Academy students have gone on field trips to Robinson & Cole, a firm that represents clients nationally and internationally, to hear about careers in law. Johnson also met with the general counsel of a large corporation based in Hartford but says it was puzzling to understand what a relationship with that company would look like.

"When I mentioned this idea of internships," recalls Johnson, "he said, 'We have a really hard time accepting second- and third-year law students as interns. I have a hard time understanding what a sixteen-year-old high school student can do.'" Johnson says that "what we want [students] to do is be around it. We want them to breathe in the air. What does it look like to work in this kind of an organization? What does it look like to be part of a high-functioning team?"

But inviting students to soak up law firm culture is not what some partners have in mind. They'd rather send speakers. But even as those offers are well-intentioned, Johnson says, having a land-use attorney talk about eminent domain won't get kids fired up—and may well have the opposite effect. Johnson recognizes that partnerships are a two-way relationship, that companies have goals, too. "For a while I had this perception that when you formed a partnership with a corporate powerhouse that they would be writing you large checks," he says. "They want good press and they want to get their people involved in doing things in the community. They want to get something out of it."

It makes intuitive sense for schools to form alliances with corporate and community organizations, but it's not always easy to do. Given pressures to improve test scores, graduation rates, student engagement, among other indicators, what is a productive partnership role? What is a waste of time? The partnering dance, says Johnson, is moving him to be more focused about how he views potential relationships. "What I really need to do is ask, 'How is this going to enrich the core of my program? How will this give teachers a chance to create an authentic learning experience?'"

Partners to Do What Districts Can't Do Alone

Large urban schools and districts can certainly benefit from well-structured and effective partnerships. But such partnerships may be even more critical in smaller urban districts with low-performing schools. This is the hidden challenge in turnaround: how to get help and attention for below-the-radar places that happen to be small. There is little glamour or national publicity to be had. Who wants to fix a school in a city that few have heard of and that may represent only several hundred students?

Yet such places need partners. Revere, Massachusetts, may not officially be the inner city, but Garfield Middle School, located along with an elementary school in a large concrete structure with a view of the Atlantic Ocean, struggles with the familiar issues of poverty and low-performance one finds five miles south in Boston. State figures show that 83 percent of Garfield students are low-income and that 54 percent do not speak English as their first language. On state tests, less than half of the sixth graders score "proficient" or above in English; only 36 percent meet that threshold in math, and, as a result, the school has not made adequate yearly progress in math for three years.

In 2009, Garfield became an "Expanded Learning Time" school, a designation that comes with an additional $1,300 per pupil in state money. The district also partnered with Citizen Schools, a nonprofit known for bringing hands-on learning and social capital experiences to middle school students. In the school turnaround environment, Citizen Schools has evolved from its roots as an afterschool program with downtown lawyers or lab scientists leading "apprenticeships" with a final product to become an end-of-day partner. The organization, which will serve 5,000 students in seven states in 2010, now has full-time teaching fellows (through a partnership with AmeriCorps) and campus directors who work to make afterschool programming complement a school's specific academic and social needs.

Despite the extra state dollars, Revere superintendent Paul Dakin says the district is stretched by a tight budget. For him, the partnership with Citizen Schools is a cost-effective way to get what he calls "wraparound services" that families need but that he can't afford to provide by hiring more staff. Dakin also realizes that because Citizen Schools has a national reputation and a large network of connections—both to top corporate and academic talent as well as to philanthropists and staff experienced in federal grant writing—they bring in turnaround resources that he might not get on his own. "They have credibility with foundations and the federal government," he says. "There seems to be more confidence in them—and I have to exploit that."

In some sense, what Garfield is getting with Citizen Schools is a partner with partners. Eric Schwarz, CEO and cofounder of Citizen Schools, says that most schools lack the capacity to build, maintain, and coordinate multiple relationships. Partnering with nonprofits like Citizen Schools, he insists, takes that piece off the plate of school leaders. "You don't have to own everything, you don't have to manage everything," says Schwarz, who testified on Capitol Hill during the reauthorization of the Elementary and Secondary Education Act and whose program has been praised as a model by the U.S. Department of Education. "We are a networked organization. We can network schools to MIT, network them to law firms, network them to big employers, network them to new talent. We even network them to their own parents."

Help with Sixth Grade (and Complicated Home Lives)

Under the extended learning time (ELT) model, students at Garfield Middle School now arrive at 7:50 a.m. and leave at 4 p.m. (two other middle schools run from 8:20 a.m. to 2:35 p.m.), with Citizen Schools running the last two hours of the day for 146 sixth graders. Plus there is optional 4–5 p.m. homework help. This has essentially divided the day into two parts. Students' core academic subjects are taught in the morning. The Citizen Schools–led afternoon is dedicated to electives, hands-on learning, academic reinforcement, tutoring, and other lessons, including character building, leadership development, and raising expectations around college and career goals.

Monica Caporale, assistant principal at Garfield Middle School, says having Citizen Schools teachers as partners—they attend staff meetings, professional development, and even dinners out with teachers—means there is "another set of people here who are involved in these children's education." Their taking on field trips and hands-on projects, like going to a courthouse and putting on a mock trial, leaves teachers to focus on core academics.

As a partner, Citizen Schools staff sees the school differently. What looks like a chore may actually be an opportunity. For example, on a February afternoon (a chicken patty and mashed potato day), Citizen Schools teacher Erin Driesbach stood near a bank of windows in the

Garfield cafeteria. While most teachers dread lunch duty, Driesbach sees it as a chance to get to know kids. "I've started making it fun for myself. You can talk with kids around the room," she points out. Sure, it is ridiculously loud and she practically screams when she reminds a student, "Don't forget to pick up your trash!" or responds that there are "five more minutes!" remaining. Mostly, she talks about college with students and shares stories of two guys from her high school that played for the Tampa Bay Buccaneers.

Citizen Schools teachers also make regular calls to parents. This is part of the organization's model, but at Garfield it has helped the school better connect with families. "Our teachers don't necessarily get the chance to call 146 sixth-grade parents," says Caporale. The calls home, made twice monthly to each of the fifteen families Citizen Schools teachers are assigned, are recorded on a "Family Engagement Tracker" chart in the group's office. They also turn in phone logs so that Citizen School leaders know the length and content of conversations. This connection paid off tangibly in the fall of 2009 when Citizen Schools hosted their trademark Wow! event and invited parents to see student work. Emily Stainer, Citizen Schools program director for Massachusetts, said the school usually had ten to fifteen families attend Back-to-School Night. She called every sixth-grade family and personally invited them the event. A stunning 200 people showed.

Communication with families—plus the fact that two Citizen Schools staffers are fluent in Spanish and one in Portuguese—has also given the school insight into home issues they may not have known about before. For example, Meredith Lowe, a first-year Citizen Schools teacher who graduated from Wesleyan in May 2009, learned through calls home why a student, Ariana, was absent from school and often exhausted when she did show up: her mother was sick and waiting for a kidney transplant. "Her mother got home at 7 P.M. from dialysis and was so tired there was no one to put her to bed," says Lowe, who alerted school counselors. Ariana's mother died in December 2009; Ariana now lives with grandparents. Lowe sees her rebounding. "She's definitely a kid who's been improving"; her grades have risen from Ds and Fs to Bs and Cs. "In the beginning of the year, she was number one on my concern list. Now she is probably number three."

The benefit to poor urban kids of being on someone's concern list cannot be overstated. As critical as such connections are, school counselors at Garfield—or at most urban schools, for that matter—don't always make them. With nearly 500 students in grades 6–8 and two counselors, guidance counselor Julie Vendittii says it's impossible to be in touch with all parents. She is grateful to have Citizen Schools building more personal relationships with students and families. "It's a great partnership. Everyone has the same goal."

Patrick Kirby, executive director of Citizen Schools' Massachusetts, says that because of the way afternoon time is structured, students get more one-on-one time with Citizen Schools staffers than they typically get from adults during the regular school day. At the same time, they are part of the school and see themselves as collaborators and supporters. "We don't come in and say, 'We are the best thing since sliced bread,'" Kirby says. "We are here to supplement. It is a humble approach. It is a conversation that is started with, 'We need to understand what your needs are.'"

Leveraging Youth and Talent

The Citizen Schools staff at Garfield, like the organization's teachers almost everywhere, is young. At twenty-eight, Megan Bird, the campus director at Garfield, is the oldest among her staff by several years. Like the corps of college graduates drawn to Teach for America and urban charter schools, Bird says her staff "gets excited about problem solving and looking at policy and fighting inequity in education and the achievement gap." Exeter- and Wellesley College–educated, Bird spent four years teaching English in Chile. Notably, she doesn't want to be a classroom teacher, but she likes working with schools and students.

Kirby contends that because Citizen School staff tends to be younger and more diverse than traditional school staffs, students forge special relationships with them. "There is something about the way we are that, frankly, makes us cool to kids," he says. He points out that "teacher likeability" opens doors to learning. This approach also offers people like Bird a way to have an intense school involvement without being an actual teacher. This is a niche that hasn't previously existed in education but that offers schools—particularly those in the midst of turnaround—a more cost-effective way to bring resources and talent to students who need more adult attention and learning time.

One thing that makes Citizen Schools cost effective for schools is that Teaching Fellows who staff campuses are actually AmeriCorps volunteers (they receive a stipend from Citizen Schools, which receives funding support from AmeriCorps). As Schwarz points out, "Our teachers aren't certified, but they are talented." The tapping of that talent and youth provides students like those at Garfield access to a mindset and social capital that they wouldn't otherwise have. And, for many parents, the distinction between who is a "real" teacher and who is a Citizen Schools teaching fellow is nonexistent.

Dawn MacDonald, a U.S Postal Service letter carrier whose daughter Regina is a sixth grader at Garfield, does not differentiate between her daughter's certified classroom teachers and her Citizen Schools teacher, Meredith Lowe. Lowe, after all, calls home and shares information about what Regina is doing. When the first call came, MacDonald admits, "I got nervous. I was like, 'What did she do?'" (She has since learned not to fear answering the phone).

MacDonald was at first reluctant to enroll Regina at Garfield. She knew it was an extended day school, and her daughter "wasn't a big fan of school" and "barely passed" fifth grade. "She was like a social butterfly. She didn't have the focus," she says, but she notes that things have turned out very differently. "Her mentality as far as school changed this year. She really tells me, 'I can't wait to go to college and get a good job.' She has an understanding that you have to do good." MacDonald says Regina understands math lessons better when Lowe does the explaining and loves the hands-on learning. "Now they are doing solar-powered cars and she did pizza making and she did some egg drop thing—whoever could build something and drop the egg off a balcony and not break it and whatever," she says. "She loves going to school."

Getting the Mix

One task in high-poverty, low-performing schools is getting students who have not done well in school to get excited about learning. Part of the fun factor for kids at Garfield Middle School is that Citizen Schools teachers are hip and young. They are sometimes also green. As a result, it took time at Garfield to get regular teachers and Citizen Schools teachers aligned on student behavior rules. Initially, says Caporale, "the first five periods were very structured, and then [kids] went to the sixth and seventh period with the Citizen Schools staff and they weren't on the same page as our teachers." Caporale says it isn't perfect, but it has improved, and the issue is really just that Citizen Schools teachers lack teaching experience.

Bird says they have been working on this but insists, "I don't see my staff struggling more than other first-year teachers." There is also a different teacher styles and cultures, she says. Where some teachers want compliance, "we invite kids into a dialogue. If they don't want to do something, we want to know why." She says part of the issue is that Citizen Schools teachers are purposefully different than classroom teachers and strive to make learning something the kids really enjoy.

It is that enjoyment that makes the partnership compelling to Revere superintendent Paul Dakin, who is less focused on what state tests will show than on keeping kids from quitting school. Middle school is "where dropout seeds are starting to sprout," says Dakin. "To see kids light up with some of the projects and exploratory learning that goes on is exciting. You know if kids are engaged and are happy, then kids will be learning."

But the bottom line is, of course, academic success. So when most sixth graders at Garfield didn't have their multiplication facts down, Citizen Schools organized a math league competition. For five months, every sixth grader spent at least an hour a week (sometimes twice a week) doing math drill contests. With this weakness in mind, when Lowe, who played varsity basketball in college, was planning her apprenticeship, she asked Garfield math teachers where students needed the most help. They told her that students were weak in understanding fractions and decimals. She decided to combine time in the gym playing basketball with time in the classroom turning shots made and missed into a math project.

"My coach in college took a lot from our statistics. We had game goals, like for field goal percentage," she says, noting that studying game stats reveals strengths and weaknesses. For the first meeting of this apprenticeship, she changed into long shorts, laced up her basketball shoes, and gathered photocopied sheets of stats from the previous night's UConn-Syracuse men's basketball game. "Statistics are far from their minds in terms of what they mean," concedes Lowe, as she heads down to meet her nineteen apprentices. But armed with enthusiasm and a good jump shot, she intends to change that. Lowe wants students to see that what they learn in school relates to the real world and that math matters. Even on the basketball court.

Use Partners to Innovate

Urban school turnaround leaders know they must think differently. And while individuals in a school or district may have imagination and ideas, Citizen Schools CEO and cofounder Eric Schwarz argues that "innovation happens faster when you bring in more outside influences and bring in partners." One key notion that Citizen Schools has pushed is the belief that students must not merely be consumers but producers of knowledge and work that is meaningful to adults. "How do you get kids producing a video game, not just playing a video game?" prods Schwarz. "How do you get them constructing a hypothesis or experiment, not just being exposed to them?"

Schwarz's argument hits a nerve. Most agree that hands-on learning is deeper and more meaningful, but how do you do that given the pressures to get students to learn more stuff faster? The idea of utterly rethinking the structure of the school experience is critical to making real advances in school turnaround, argues Andrew Calkins, senior program officer at the Stupsky Foundation. Calkins says everything has to be on the table, and schools need to find ways to more intimately engage students, to make learning more "personalized," to blend in- and out-of-class experiences, which reorders the learning day and considers a student's learning style.

To be sure, there is a lot of good thinking and testing of new ideas happening right now. Innovation feels risky, and there is a view that "experimenting" with urban kids' education is unseemly. But protests sound less credible in the face of repeated failure. Schwarz's point about partners—and he is certainly not the only one voicing this view—is that accelerating our learning about what works (and what doesn't) is critical right now. Schools cannot do everything themselves and expect to do it well. Partnerships need to have a purpose. They need to be well articulated. But they can offer turnaround schools new ideas and much-needed help at a critical moment.

7

THERE IS NO FINISH LINE

W HEN YOU STEP INSIDE A SCHOOL in the midst of turnaround, you know it. There are, of course, the physical signs: libraries with books still in boxes, talk of innovative spaces (mock courtrooms, computer labs, etc.), and plans for painted murals.

But there is also a special kind of urgent energy manifested in the explosive, brainstorming way that school leaders and teachers speak about what they are doing. They are alive and engaged in their work and, at the same time, scared that it could all fail. They are thinking about radically different things at once: pedagogy, teamwork, collaboration, public policy, social justice, and why a smart student shows up late every single day not wearing dress code footwear. *What is so hard about black shoes?!*

These schools are exciting places to be. At the same time, one wonders if years from now it all will have seemed more like the staging of a Broadway show than the deep change that we and, more pointedly, students in high-poverty schools need.

Despite the high-drama combination of bright hope and grating uncertainty that characterize this moment, education is not really an all-or-nothing deal. Failing schools must make huge leaps quickly, and whether or not this happens will shape public policy and support for educational initiatives in the future. So it feels like a high-stakes enterprise. But the question of what can be learned from what is being tried is a separate matter. Even in schools that are closed, there are good ideas. In successful schools, there are opportunities to do better.

This is not to minimize the urgency of now but, instead, to bring perspective to the challenge. As Mark Oakman, the Vietnam vet turned chemistry teacher at High School, Inc., in Hartford observed, just because you have not met the standard does not mean you've failed. It just means you're not done yet. There are ideas to be taken and lessons learned from what is unfolding now, regardless of how it turns out or is ultimately judged.

One of the worries about turnaround is that there is simply too much to achieve. Even Scott Given, whose nonprofit UP Schools are involved in district turnaround, has doubts about what can actually be achieved. "I'm very concerned about the broader school turnaround movement, because the human capital and organizational capital is not poised to drive fast school turnaround at scale," says Given. "There is all this political and financial capital emphasis on turnaround schools right now. I think, unfortunately, a lot of the efforts will fall flat, and within five years the idea of school turnaround will have fizzled."

While Given's warning might be interpreted as a reason not to pursue change, it can also been viewed as an argument for considering school-level work. A lot of discussion has centered on sweeping citywide initiatives and district-level reforms, but the school building may be the unit that determines the viability of good ideas. It may be the most concrete place to record results of the current effort. The best scenario for reform is support all the way down the line—from state to district to school to principals to teachers. But is that realistic? Is that possible?

Culture First (Beware of the Implementation Dip)

For school leaders who begin turnaround work, there are competing approaches to consider and different strategies to try. How can you know what is worth pursing and what should be discarded? How do you know if you on the right track? Justin Cohen, president of the School Turnaround Group at Mass Insight, cautions that because top-to-bottom change is so disruptive, schools can "look like a disaster" even as they move in the right direction. "We call it the implementation dip," he says. "You have to relentlessly communicate that there will be painful things to go through." Yet, signs that appear negative may reflect change under way. For example, in early stages of turnaround schools have more student suspensions; and while teacher attendance rises, student attendance rates often fall. Cohen says this happens because administrators start enforcing rules around student behavior, dress code, and student-student and student-teacher interactions that improve the school climate. It can be difficult in the moment to stick with the agenda, he says, but it pays off. Even if more students are suspended at first, "if you have a culture where it is unacceptable to say shit in the hallways, you won't have fights physically."

One of the first steps in school turnaround, regardless of the model, is to recast expectations. "In a broken school, you need to change the school culture," says Given. "You need to change the culture from low expectations and mediocrity, a culture of disrespect into a culture of urgency, high expectations, no excuses." Given turned around the poor-performing Excel Academy Charter School in East Boston to make it the state's top middle school test performer by starting with a very structured environment, one that sets rules for behavior right down to what to do if your pencil breaks ("Simply lift your pencil into the air in your left hand and a teacher will come and replace it with one that is fully sharpened.").

He maintains that spending time and effort up front creates a climate in which everyone knows what is expected and what to do. It also makes better use of time. "How many times in a school day, a school week, a year, does a pencil break? If you can get rid of these opportunities for distraction, you can focus on driving excellent instruction and learning." But while school culture sets the tone, Given says his first "early win" at Excel happened to be about numbers: when he got results of student benchmark assessments and saw that his students were making gains similar to those at other schools in the same charter network. Not everyone will record a numbers victory right away, but ultimately, say both Given and Cohen, it needs to be about test results. "There have to be score increases," says Cohen. "I don't care if the test is imperfect, scores have to go up. They have to go up by twenty-five percentage points. If you were at 10 percent you need to be at 35 percent at the end of year three."

Just four months after opening High School, Inc. (too soon for test results), principal Terrell Hill described the moment when he realized that some things were working. As the result of a troubling encounter, he saw that students were getting his get-serious-about-school message. After essentially being forced to enroll two tenth graders who had been serving jail time, he left a meeting in his school conference room with an earnest Catholic Charities representative "knowing [the students] weren't serious, that they were just acting." But, he said, he "had no intention of not admitting them or welcoming them to the school." After the meeting, the two new students went to the cafeteria and greeted kids they had known in grade school. Within minutes, Hill had four students in his office. "Do you know those kids?" they asked. Hill responded that he didn't but that they were enrolling at the school. "They said, 'Those kids don't belong here. They are not our type of kid.'"

It was that phrase "our type of kid" that told Hill he was building a culture with a strong, positive identity. And when twenty-seven of the thirty-one students who made the first-semester honor roll (no more than one C) were ninth graders, Hill noted that students who had signed onto his program from the starting point—as opposed to those who dropped into the school in tenth grade because they had no other high school plans—were buying his program.

The Elusive Goal of College Attendance

School culture is critical. Test scores matter. But at the heart of turnaround—especially at schools like the Law and Government Academy—is the big-minded press for the American dream of a college education.

Law and Government Academy guidance counselor Charlene Senteio is a one-woman department in a school of 400 students whose needs reach far beyond help with college essays. And although her office looks like a festival of opportunity, with colorful felt college banners and posters of dappled campuses, the reality is more sober.

The truth is that, despite all the talk of college, many students struggle to even be accepted. And many fewer, not just at this school but from high-poverty schools across the country, ever actually attend. Still fewer earn a degree. Despite the Law and Government Academy's academically oriented theme, by April it appears that of the eighty-five students who applied to four-year colleges for the 2009–2010 school year, only forty received admissions offers. Principal Adam Johnson is hoping that thirty will actually enroll.

As the May 1 decision deadline approaches, students wrestle with options—in this case not about which college to attend but whether to or not to go at all. They stare at financial aid packages with gaps they cannot fathom how to fill. Even the best at Law and Government Academy, those whose future jobs might justify a financial risk, see a few thousand dollars (reasonable by middle-class standards) as insurmountable. "When you are the first in the family to go to college, when you are living not paycheck to paycheck but minimum credit card payment to minimum credit card payment, even making up a gap of $3,000 seems impossible," says Johnson. And even if they wanted to borrow for college, "many are not creditworthy."

As the school year leans into its final stretch, Johnson is frustrated about the college piece of his school's turnaround mission. "I don't want my kids to go to Capital Community College," he says, citing studies showing high-poverty students are more likely to succeed if they attend a four-year college immediately following high school. "I want kids getting full rides to Providence College. I want kids getting accepted to Smith, Mount Holyoke, Colby, and Bates. I hope I have a couple of kids who apply to Harvard, but I want kids who legitimately consider deciding between Boston College and Emerson, weighing that they are both in Boston but different. I want kids to have that type of decision-making power."

Right now, that seems astonishingly far off. Johnson said that in 2009–2010, only a few students scored more than 400 points on any portion of the SAT, making it unlikely that a top college would extend the sort of financial aid they would need to attend such schools. Instead, they are left being accepted to colleges with extremely low admission criteria but with annual costs of $35,000 or more.

Senteio says it is difficult to make kids understand the difference between colleges. "They are not into the hierarchy or the prestige of certain schools. It is very difficult to convince a kid to go through the extra hoop" required to apply to more competitive institutions, she says, noting that students apply to the University of Bridgeport "because they have an easy application." They are just happy to be accepted at a four-year college.

So, as Johnson looks at the work ahead of him, it is not just about meeting state graduation standards (a tall order at this moment) but about changing how students view themselves and their education. It is about better strategies as well as about getting students in a position to have choices. At present, he is frustrated that many students "are not working hard enough." He wonders aloud what the problem is. Have they been so conditioned to sit and take standardized tests that they have no idea what they are aiming for or how to think critically? Lately, he has been entertaining many theories. Are his kids consuming too much sugar, making them lethargic? Teachers tell him that students know how to do the work, but he hears from them that "they just give up so easily." Johnson wonders if they feel as if the system has failed them so there is no point in engaging. "Why does a person choose not to vote?" he asks.

Keeping at Change

The strong government push to make the worst schools better within a three-year window of committed federal funding and attention has fostered an explosion of experimentation and a willingness for districts, schools, teachers to try—and try again. And that is what Johnson is aiming to do.

"We have to rework our strategy," says Johnson, who has already been interviewing for another school counselor and has stepped up student visits to college campuses. He's also planning a college tour himself to meet with leaders and sell them on his kids. In addition, Christina Kishimoto, assistant superintendent for school design, said they recently decided that having a Freshman Academy at Hartford Public High School wasn't working. It put too much pressure on grades 10–12 schools to quickly prepare students for state graduation tests and was not enough time to "start a new culture" among incoming students. According to her, as of the 2011–2012 school year, ninth graders will enroll at the other three academies, including the Law and Government Academy.

This level of comfort with midstream course change may end up being one of the most lasting results of school turnaround. Yet, even if the pedantic pace of school reform gets a serious nudge, it's unlikely that the headline of turnaround—the bad-to-great transformation of schools—will happen as quickly as hoped. It may be more possible at the lower grades, but at high school, as Johnson's challenges suggest, there is a lot of academic catch-up and culture change to do. The good news, observes Kishimoto, is that work the district began two years ago on strengthening eighth-grade reading programs is beginning to pay off. "Those eighth graders are now ninth graders. They are better prepared," she says. "The tenth graders were just before reform."

The numbers, no doubt, will tell the story. "I think we will see a difference in next year's CAPT scores," Kishimoto says with a clear tone of anticipation. Although test scores matter—a lot—they do not represent a finish line that is reached. Johnson says he will measure his school's success by CAPT scores as well as by college acceptances, enrollments, surveys of school climate, and how well regarded they are by parents who are choosing schools for their children. What will be the buzz on Law and Government Academy?

Law and Government Academy guidance counselor Senteio says students she speaks with are not yet making their choices based on academics and personal goals. "They choose the academy based on who has to wear what uniform. "Or, 'Where is my friend going?' Some kids say, 'I am not coming to Law and Government Academy because I don't want to wear a tie.' I have asked kids point-blank, and I hear, 'Such and such a teacher I hear is really, really nice.' Are they making a decision based on curriculum? Not yet."

There is a lot to change in order to turn around a school. There are worries—about what happens when federal stimulus money runs out, if budgets get cut, if students don't go to college and come back to tell others that it can be done, if kids don't work or believe, if teachers don't move them ahead fast enough. But there are also dreams. Johnson imagines a stand-alone Law and Government Academy serving students in grades 6–12, "and we become a choice where families hold us in as high regard as the magnets."

Turnaround, as schools like Law and Government Academy suggest, is not a result but a process. It is a dynamic undertaking in which worries and dreams are partners in the pursuit. And there is, by definition, no endpoint.

Working on Little Rocks

Hartford's High School, Inc., and Law and Government Academy are in the tumultuous middle of turnaround, trying to chart a course and figure out what works. So what does it look like when you've made it past the three-year mark? Even schools that have found turnaround success have challenges to address. They are just different challenges.

According to several measures (daily attendance, test scores, a 98 percent graduation rate, popularity among families choosing schools), Withrow University High School in Cincinnati—where 96 percent of students are minorities, 18 percent have disabilities, and 59 percent are poor—is a turnaround success. While Principal Sharon Johnson appreciates the strong reviews, she sees a lot of work remaining. "Are we effective? Yes. But no, I don't consider us an excellent school," she says. The test scores are good: in 2008–2009, 93 percent of students passed state graduation tests in reading, 84 percent in math, 95 percent in writing, 89 percent in science, and 92 percent in social studies.

But the scores, she says, "are not where I want them to be." She wants a stronger science showing. "In science, I have not successfully turned that around. Have I made gains? Yes. Have I made enough gains? No, not by my standards," she says. And while test results for the school represent students who passed in either tenth or eleventh grade, she wants more passing the first time around and wants results "in the high 90s in every area." And while students all graduate and each year about 85 percent apply to college, just 70 percent actually enroll. And Johnson is not sure how well they do once they get there.

According to Johnson, the difference between the first few years of turnaround and now is that "I'm not working on big rocks now. I am working on smaller rocks." While smaller rocks can become bigger rocks—small problems can fester or dips can become slides—Johnson says there is a certain level of pride among teachers and students who have become acclimated to working at a particular level with particular results. But, she says, "you have to work to sustain it," and that includes looking for areas to improve and reminding people about goals. "You are dealing with human nature," she says, noting that she spends time making sure "there is consistency and continuity" in the little things.

For example, she wants professional development time to be used to make improvements. One of her concerns is college readiness and performance. State reports show that while 92 percent of students take the ACT, that the mean composite score is only 16, with tables showing that means that only 20 percent of U.S. students taking the test scored lower.

Because she is concerned about how well curriculum does, or doesn't, prepare students to perform well on the ACT, she wanted teachers on an upcoming professional development day to see how ACT content areas aligned with class teaching. Johnson says she met with resistance: "They wanted to use the time to look at some of the exams they have given to see what they need to go back and rework. I was hoping they would do that as a team meeting and not on their PD day."

Johnson pushes teachers hard. But she didn't want this difference to become "a big rock," so she met part way: they could spend half of the day going over old exams and the rest looking at the ACT matchup. Part of sustaining a well-functioning school is seeking improvement even when you are already pretty good. But that also requires managing people and knowing when to stand firm and when to relent. "There are some things I will compromise on, and some things I will not compromise on," says Johnson. "Some people say, 'Sharon you are just unreasonable,' but my standards will not change because we haven't gotten there yet."

Reaching Deeper and Longer

At Taft Information Technology High School, it has been nearly a decade, but, in Principal Anthony G. Smith's mind, school turnaround is not done yet. Each September the students who enter his school still arrive with needs that are as big and deep as they have ever been. That has not changed. And, in fact, it has pushed Smith to think about what more his school can do. How can he bring more positive influence to bear in their lives?

Although not a big athlete himself, Smith has started using sports participation, and the requirement that players meet academic eligibility requirements, to drive students to work harder inside the classroom and out. He believes that it's also another vehicle for giving students more meaningful relationships and guidance from adults. Before the turnaround, only thirty students participated in sports; today, half of the 485-student body is on sports teams or involved in other cocurricular activities. They now have three football teams, six basketball teams, softball, baseball, track and field, and girls rowing ("We had to teach the girls to swim first," notes Smith). Part of the afterschool schedule for athletes, explains Smith, is an organized study table (much like many colleges have for NCAA athletes) staggered between girls' and boys' teams. His goal is to keep them at school, focused, and safe, until at least 6 P.M.

Smith is also about to launch another source of support. He is working with a nearby culinary school on his plan to add dinner to the afterschool day. His belief about student success is straightforward: "You have to build relationships with these kids and let them know you care about what happens to them." While Smith had the benefit of transforming Taft at a moment when there was no clock ticking in the background marking off three years, that is not the case today. Certainly, he understood that he needed dramatic change quickly, but there is a difference between *change* and *test score results*.

Still, the lesson that both Smith and Sharon Johnson of Withrow University High School bring to bear on the present turnaround movement is the understanding that test scores don't change without serious support for students. It is not just about fixing instruction or revamping curriculum; it's also about guiding students who may not have a lot of guidance or support outside of the school building. And, as both demonstrate, there are always things needing improvement.

Quiet Hallways

It is not clear—and may not be for a few years—whether Hartford Public High School is actually being turned around. In the district's language, the school was "redesigned" and split into four smaller high schools. While one of those, the Freshman Academy, will be phased out, the others—including the Law and Government Academy, the Nursing Academy, and the Academy of Engineering and Green Technology—face a test: can they dramatically change the game for students?

Senior nursing student Shaquana Cochran started at the school when it was still a single Hartford Public High School. A vocal and opinionated young woman dressed in blue scrubs (the nursing school's uniform), Cochran is not sure if redesign is working. But she does notice fewer fights among students in the hallways. Carlanna Dyer, a senior at the Law and Government Academy, agrees, though she's not entirely pleased. "Before, it was loud, it was crazy," she says. "I'm not going to lie. It was fun. Not because of the whole fighting thing, but because everybody was like, 'Ohhh whaat's up! Oh I know you!' Now it's just quiet."

Quiet may be one sound of progress in the rebirth of failing inner-city schools, but another is surely how students describe their futures. Cochran slips in phrases like "when I go to college" and is quick to boast about hours of homework and requirements of nursing. "I swear I slacked my freshman year," she admits, "I barely passed. I had a D average. My sophomore year I went up a little."

As seven students gathered in a school conference room to talk for nearly two hours one afternoon about the changes they see, it is obvious that school turnaround is not only about structures and conditions and policy moves designed to have impact. It is also about a population of students trying to think differently about themselves. While there are some who were always destined to succeed—like Law and Government Academy senior Danny Contreras, who arrived from Puerto Rico in seventh grade and taught himself English grammar from textbooks (and who borrows a book on computer programming language from a conference room bookshelf after the conversation ends)—many more are trying to figure out if they have a future beyond the failure that pervades their daily lives. It is not easy work. Cochran gets angry when her eleven-year-old brother comes home crying that a teacher has said he won't amount to anything. And the news on TV, she says, tells how troubled the city is, how bad the schools are. "You feel like, 'I got to join in the statistic,'" she says. "Sometimes I feel like giving up."

When Hartford Public High School was redesigned, Cochran came to the nursing program and left behind friends to start a turnaround of her own. It has not been a straight line of ascent. She thought about quitting school earlier in the year but grew close to an English teacher whom she credits with helping her through a crisis. Now she is taking a community college biology course taught by a University of Connecticut professor and expressing annoyance at kids who come to *her* school and think they can fool around.

Shaquana Cochran may not be the measure of school turnaround success that education leaders and policy makers look to, but she provides very real hope. If reformers will hang in long enough—not just to satisfy a bump in scores but to earn the trust of those being asked to work and achieve differently than they were asked to do in the past— then they may see signs of better schools and better lives. After years of doing poorly, Cochran glimpses possibility. "When I start seeing those As and Bs, my heart starts fluttering like butterflies," she says. "Like I can do it."

RESOURCES

Achievement First. *Professional Growth Plan*. Internally published document. New Haven, CT: Achievement First, 2009-2010. 1–10.

Adamowski, Steven. "School Redesign: Lessons from Hartford." PowerPoint presentation at The Education Trust, November 12, 2009, Washington, DC.

Ahmed, Azam. "Schools Get Turned Around—and Around and Around." *Chicago Tribune,* August 17, 2009. http://articles.chicagotribune.com/ 2009-08-17/news/0908160424_1_chicago-public-schools-elementary-low-performing.

Anderson, Amy Berk, and Dale DeCesare. "Opening Closed Doors: Lessons from Colorado's First Independent Charter School." Denver, CO: Audenblick, Palaich, 2006.

Anderson, Nick. "U.S. Devises Scoring System for School Reform." *Washington Post*, November 12, 2009, A3.

Anderson, Nick, and Bill Turque. "15 States, D.C., Make First Cut in Race to the Top School Reform Contest." *Washington Post*, March 5, 2010. http://www.washingtonpost.com/wp-dyn/content/article/2010/03/04/ AR2010030402262.html.

Barbic, Chris, and Mike Feinberg. "Grier Has Opened Door to System of Great Schools." *Houston Chronicle.* March 10, 2010. http://www.chron.com/displ/ story.mpl/editorial/outlook/6907280.html.

Bass, Paul. "Teachers Give Tough Grades—to Themselves." *New Haven Independent.* January 29, 2010. http://newhavenindependent.org/index.php/ archives/entry/teachers_grade_themselves_tough/.

Berry, Barnett, Diana Montgomery, Rachel Curtis, Mindy Hernandez, Judy Wurtzel, and Jon Snyder. *Creating and Sustaining Urban Teacher Residencies: A New Way to Recruit, Prepare, and Retain Effective Teachers in High-Needs Districts*. Washington, DC: Aspen Institute; Hillsborough, NC: Center for Teaching Quality, 2008.

Blanks, Jasmine, Naima Bashir, and Joe Nathan. "Collaborating for Success: Lessons for Public Schools." Report produced by the Center for School Change, Macalester College, St. Paul, MN, March 2010. 33–34.

Borman, Geoffrey D. *The Past, Present, and Future of Comprehensive School Reform*. Washington, DC: Center for Comprehensive School Reform and Improvement, 2009.

Brinson, Dana, and Lauren Morando Rhim. *Breaking the Habit of Low Performance: Successful School Restructuring Stories*. Lincoln, IL: Academic Development Institute, 2009.

Calkins, Andrew, William Guenther, Grace Belfiore, and David Lash. *The Turnaround Challenge*. Boston: Mass Insight Education and Research Institute, 2007.

Childress, Stacey, Geoff Marietta, and Sara Suchman. *Boston Teacher Residency: Developing a Strategy for Long-Term Impact*. Case Study 9-309-043. Cambridge, MA: Harvard Business School, 2008.

City, Elizabeth A. *Resourceful Leadership: Tradeoff and Tough Decisions on the Road to School Improvement*. Cambridge, MA: Harvard Education Press, 2008.

Coleman, James S. "Social Capital in the Creation of Human Capital." *American Journal of Sociology* 94, supp. (1988): S95–S120.

—. *Equality of Educational Opportunity (Coleman) Study (EEOS)*. 1966. Ann Arbor, MI: Inter-University Consortium for Political and Social Research, 2007. doi:10.3886/ICPSR06389.

Cruz, Gilbert. "Can Charter-School Execs Help Failing Public Schools?" *Time*, June 27, 2009. http://www.time.com/time/nation/article/0,8599,1907203,00.html.

de la Torre, Marisa, and Julia Gwynne. *When Schools Close: Effects on Displaced Students in Chicago Public Schools*. Chicago: University of Chicago Urban Education Institute, 2009.

Denver Public Schools. "CSAP Results Mixed: Elementary Schools Show Gains, Cole Middle School Transition Will Receive 'Full Support' of District." News release. August 2, 2004.

de Souza Briggs, Xavier. "Brown Kids in White Suburbs: Housing Mobility and the Many Faces of Social Capital." *Housing Policy Debate* 9, no. 1 (1998): 177–221.

DiFilippo, Dana. "High Schools Could Specialize." *Cincinnati Enquirer,* January 12, 1999, B1.

Dillon, Sam. "U.S. Effort to Reshape Schools Faces Challenges." *New York Times*, June 1, 2009. http://www.nytimes.com/2009/06/02/education/02educ.html.

—. "Dangling $4.3 Billion, Obama Pushes States to Shift on Education." *New York Times*, August 17, 2009, A1.

—. "After Criticism, the Administration Is Praised for Final Rules on Education Grants." *New York Times,* November 12, 2009, A18.

—. "Education Grant Effort Faces Late Opposition." *New York Times*, January 19, 2010, A20.

Duke, Daniel. "What We Know and Don't Know About Improving Low-Performing Schools." *Phi Delta Kappan* 87 (June 2006): 729–734.

Duncan, Arne. "Turning Around the Bottom 5 Percent." Address at the National Alliance for Public Charter Schools Conference, June 22, 2009, Washington, DC. http://www2.ed.gov/news/speeches/2009/06/06222009.html.

Elliott, Scott. "The School Reform Divide." *Dayton Daily News*, November 17, 2005. http://www.daytondailynews.com/blogs/content/shared-gen/blogs/dayton/education/entries/2005/11/17/some_of_the_big.html.

Elmore, Richard F. *School Reform from the Inside Out.* Cambridge, MA: Harvard Education Press, 2004.

—. "I Used to Think . . . and Now I Think . . ." *Harvard Education Letter* 26, no. 1 (2010): 8.

Fairbanks, Amanda M. "Gauging the Dedication of Teacher Corps Grads." *New York Times*, January 4, 2010, A10.

Fischer, Ben. "New CPS Chief Better Bring a Cape." *Cincinnati Enquirer,* March 26, 2008, A1.

—. "Popular Interim Chief Said to Be Front Runner for Job." *Cincinnati Enquirer,* January 12, 2009, A1.

Gaston, Alonzo, Sonja Kelley, Kathleen Knight Abowitz, Kate Rousmaniere, and William Solomon. *Collaboration Within and Without: The Case Study of Taft High School.* Columbus: Ohio State Department of Education; Toronto: Ontario Institute for Studies in Education, 1999.

Gewertz, Catherine. "Duncan's Call for School Turnaround Sparks Debate." *Education Week*, August 11, 2009. http://www.edweek.org/login. html?source=http://www.edweek.org/ew/articles/2009/07/21/37turnaround. h28.html&destination=http://www.edweek.org/ew/articles/2009/07/21/ 37turnaround.h28.html&levelId=2100.

Glazerman, Steven, Dan Goldhaber, Susanna Loeb, Douglas O. Staiger, and Grover J. Whitehurst. *America's Teacher Corps*. Washington, DC: Brookings Institution, 2010.

Goode, Steven, and Jeffrey B. Cohen. "Hartford Superintendent Says Reports of Gangs at School Inaccurate." *Hartford Courant*, October 20, 2009. http:// www.allbusiness.com/government/government-bodies-offices-regional/ 13260210-1.html.

Gordon, Robert, Thomas J. Kane, and Douglas O. Staiger. *Identifying Effective Teachers Using Performance on the Job*. Washington, DC: Brookings Institution, 2006.

Harris, Wendy. "Who's Applying? Potential Turnaround Managers." *The Notebook*, February 2010. http://www.thenotebook.org/february-2010/102173/ whos-applying-potential-turnaround-managers.

Hassel, Bryan C., and Daniela Doyle. *The Tab: How Connecticut Can Fix Its Dysfunctional Education Spending System to Reward Success, Incentivize Choice and Boost Student Achievement*. New Haven: Connecticut Coalition for Achievement Now; Chapel Hill, NC: Public Impact, 2009.

Hawthorne, Michael. "Taft Priority: Education." *Cincinnati Enquirer*, January 20, 2000, A1.

Haynes, Mariana. *State Strategies for Turning Around Low-Performing Schools and Districts*. Arlington, VA: National Association of State Boards of Education, 2007.

Helliwell, John F., and Robert D. Putnam. "Education and Social Capital." *Eastern Economic Journal* 33, no. 1 (2007): 1–19.

Henig, Jeffrey. "What Do We Know About the Outcomes of KIPP Schools?" East Lansing, MI: Great Lakes Center for Education Research and Practice, 2008.

Hill, Paul, Christine Campbell, David Menefee-Libey, Brianna Dusseault, Michael DeArmond, and Bethany Gross. *Portfolio School Districts for Big Cities: An Interim Report*. Seattle: Center on Reinventing Public Education, 2009.

"Innovations Must Continue." Editorial. *Cincinnati Enquirer*, June 25, 2002, B10.

Kahlenberg, Richard D. "Turnaround Schools That Work." *Education Week*, September 2, 2009, 28.

Kamau, Pius. "Dedication Beyond Protest." *Denver Post*, June 28, 2006, A1.

King, Neil Jr. "Obama Wins a Battle as a Teacher's Union Shows Flexibility." *Wall Street Journal*, October 17, 2009, A3.

Kowal, Julie, Emily Ayscue Hassel, and Bryan C. Hassel. *Successful School Turnarounds: Seven Steps for District Leaders*. Washington, DC: Center for Comprehensive School Reform and Improvement, 2009.

Learning Point Associates. *Turnarounds with New Leaders and Staff*. Naperville, IL: Learning Point Associates, 2005.

—. "Newsletter: District Support of School Improvement: Highlights from Three Districts." Washington, DC: The Center for Comprehensive School Reform and Improvement, 2009.

Liu, Edward, Susan Moore Johnson, and Heather G. Peske. "New Teachers and the Massachusetts Signing Bonus: The Limits of Inducements." *Educational Evaluation and Policy Analysis* 26, no. 3 (2004): 217–236.

McNamara Horvat, Erin, Elliot B. Weininger, and Annette Lareau. "From Social Ties to Social Capital: Class Differences in the Relations Between Schools and Parent Networks." *American Educational Research Journal* 40, no. 2 (2003): 319–351.

McNeil, Michele. "'Race to Top' Guidelines Stress Use of Test Data." *Education Week*, July 23, 2009. http://www.edweek.org/login.html?source=http://www.edweek.org/ew/articles/2009/07/23/37race.h28.html&destination=http://www.edweek.org/ew/articles/2009/07/23/37race.h28.html&levelId=2100.

Merritt, Grace E. "Initiative Takes Aim at Connecticut's Persistent School Achievement Gap." *Hartford Courant*, November 18, 2009. http://articles.courant.com/2009-11-18/news/09111712259575_1_focus-on-achievement-gap-white-students-hispanic-students.

Mintrop, Heinrich, and Gail L. Sunderman. "Predictable Failure of Federal Sanctions-Driven Accountability for School Improvement—and Why We May Retain It Anyway." *Educational Researcher* 38, no. 5 (2009): 353–364.

Mrozowski, Jennifer. "Adamowski Highlights Progress in Cincinnati." *Cincinnati Enquirer*, October 4, 2001, B8.

—. "Superintendent's Departure a Surprise." *Cincinnati Enquirer*, June 25, 2002, A1.

—. "School Tries Single-Gender Classes to Boost Learning." *Cincinnati Enquirer*, November 12, 2002, A1.

—. "Stories from Inside Run-Down Schools." *Cincinnati Enquirer*, April 30, 2003, A6.

Nathan, Joe. "How Cincinnati Turned its Schools Around and What Other Systems Can Learn from It." *Education Week*, January 9, 2008, 24.

Nelson, Libby. "Duncan Urges Colleges to Help Underperforming Schools More." *Chronicle of Higher Education*, September 10, 2009. http://chronicle.com/article/Duncan-Urges-Colleges-to-Help/48358/.

Otterman, Sharon. "A Judge Blocks the City from Closing 19 Underperforming Schools." *New York Times*, March 27, 2010, A15.

Peterson, Molly. "KIPP: Learning a Lesson from Big Business." *Bloomberg Businessweek*, February 4, 2010. http://www.businessweek.com/magazine/content/10_07/b4166056302366.htm.

Podgursky, Michael J., and Matthew G. Springer. *Teacher Performance Pay: A Review*. Nashville, TN: National Center on Performance Initiatives, 2006.

"Q&A with Dr. Steven Adamowski." *Cincinnati Enquirer*, July 14, 2002. http://www.enquirer.com.http://www.enquirer.com/editions/2002/07/14/loc_q_a_with_dr_steven.html.

"Rallies Across California Decry High-Education Funding Cuts." *Los Angeles Times,* March 4, 2010. http://latimesblogs.latimes.com/lanow/2010/03.

Rourke, James, and Elizabeth Boone. "Withrow University High School: Every Student College Bound." *Principal Leadership* 10 (June 2009): 44–47.

Roza, Marguerite, Dan Goldhaber, and Paul T. Hill. "The Productivity Imperative: Getting More Benefits from School Costs in an Era of Tight Budgets." *Education Week*, January 7, 2009, 34.

Roza, Marguerite, and Sarah Yatzo. *Beyond Teacher Reassignments: Better Ways Districts Can Remedy Salary Inequities Across Schools*. Seattle: Center on Reinventing Public Education, 2010.

Rivero, Victor. "Turning Around Schools in Need." Districtadministration. com, September 2009. http://www.districtadministration.com/viewarticle .aspx?articleid=2118.

Rivkin, Steven G., Eric A. Hanushek, and John F. Kain. "Teachers, Schools, and Academic Achievement." *Econometra* 73, no. 2 (2005): 417–458.

Rotella, Carlo. "Class Warrior." *New Yorker*, February 1, 2010, 24.

Sanders, William L., and June C. Rivers. *Cummulative and Residual Effects of Teachers on Future Student Academic Achievement.* Knoxville: University of Tennessee Value-Added Research and Assessment Center, 1996.

Silva, Elena. "Teachers at Work: Improving Teacher Quality Through Design." *Education Sector Reports*. October, 2009. http://www.educationsector.org/ usr_doc/Teachers_at_Work.pdf.

Smarick, Andy. "The Turnaround Fallacy." *Education Next* 10 (Winter 2010). http://educationnext.org/the-turnaround-fallacy/.

Spencer, Mark. "Standardized Math Tests Show State's Economic, Ethnic Disparities Persist." *Hartford Courant*, October 15, 2009. http://articles.courant. com/2009-10-15/news/national-report-card-1015.art_1_standardized-test-results-gap-between-white-students.

Steiner, Lucy. *Tough Decisions: Closing Persistently Low-Performing Schools.* Lincoln, IL: Academic Development Institute, 2009.

Tortora, Andrea. "Education Chief Calls Parham Model School." *Cincinnati Enquirer,* July 14, 2000, C2.

Truscheit, Tori. *Connecticut's Teachers, Principals and Race to the Top.* New Haven: Connecticut Coalition for Achievement Now, 2010.

Vaznis, James. "Boston Gets an F in Teacher Appraisals." *Boston Globe*, February 23, 2010, A1.

—. "Dramatic Shake-Up Planned at 12 Boston Public Schools." *Boston Globe*, March 5, 2010, A1.

—. "Union Blasts City Schools Overhaul Plan." *Boston Globe*, April 13, 2010, A1.

Viadero, Debra. "Research Doesn't Offer Much Guidance on Turnarounds." *Education Week*, August 12, 2009, 10.

Weingarten, Randi, "A New Path Forward: Four Approaches to Quality Teaching and Better Schools." Speech delivered at the National Press Club, January 12, 2010, Washington, DC. http://aft.3cdn.net/227d12e668432ca48e_twm6b90k1.pdf.

Wilson, David McKay. "Incent This! Competition Drives Federal Ed Reforms at Every Level." *Harvard Education Letter* 26, no. 1 (2010). http://www.hepg.org/hel/article/439.

Yeager, Margery. *Stiff Armed: No Child Left Behind's Unused Funding Flexibility.* Washington, DC: Education Sector, 2007.

Government Sources and Documents

2009 National Assessment of Educational Progress. http://nces.ed.gov/nationasreportcard/.

Blue Ribbon Schools Program, 2010 Application. OMB Control Number, 1860-0506. Found at Robert A. Taft Informational Technology High School, Cincinnati, OH.

Collective Bargaining Agreement Between the Hartford Board of Education and the Hartford Federation of Teachers, Local 1018, AFT, AFL-CIO, July 1, 2008–June 30, 2011. http://ct.aft.org/1018/index.cfm?action=article&articleID=7dedd448-8f66-4afa-b703-df18fea4cb52.

ConnCAN Data Chart. http://www.conncan.org/sites/default/files/research/2009_NAEP_Reading_Results_0.pdf.

Coopersmith, Jared, and Kerry Gruber. "Characteristics of Public, Private, and Bureau of Indian Education Elementary and Secondary School Teachers in the United States: Results from the 2007–08 Schools and Staffing Survey." NCES-324, table 3, p. 9. U.S. Department of Education, June 2009.

Duncan, Arne. Press conference call, FY2011 budget request. February 1, 2010, 1:30 P.M. ET.

Lohman, Judith. "State Funding for Interdistrict Magnet Schools." *OLR Research Report.* 2010-R-0056. Office of Legislative Research, State of Connecticut. March 9, 2010. http://www.cga.ct.gov/2010/rpt/2010-R-0056.htm.

National Center for Education Statistics. "Revenues for Public Elementary and Secondary Schools, by Source of Funds: Selected Years 1919–20 through 2006–2007. *Digest of Education Statistics.* http://nces.ed.gov/programs/digest/d09/tables/dt09_172.asp.

New Haven Board of Education and the New Haven Federation of Teachers, Local 933. Contract July 1, 2010–June 30, 2014. Appendix A: Turnaround Schools. http://www.nhps.net/sites/default/files/Appendix_A-Turnaround_Schools_00275511_3_0_0.pdf. October 2, 2009.

New York City Department of Education. "Quality Review Report: South Shore High School, High School 515." By Rev. Peter Lewis. October 11–13, 2006. http://schools.nyc.gov/OA/SchoolReports/2006-07/Quality_Review_2007_K515.pdf.

—. "Building Condition Assessment Survey 2008-2009: Architectural Inspection, South Shore HS—K, 6565 Flatlands Avenue, Brooklyn, NY 11236." April 14, 2009. http://schools.nycenet.edu/documents/SCA/enc_rpts/K515_A.pdf.

Rutzick, Karen. "Nation's Report Card Finds CT Achievement Gap Still Country's Worst." Press release, Conn CAN. March 24, 2010. http://www.conncan.org/ media/nations-report-card-finds-ct-achievement-gap-still-countrys-worst.

U.S. Department of Education. "Obama Administration Announces Historic Opportunity to Turn Around Nation's Lowest-Achieving Public Schools." Press release, Department of Education. August 26, 2009. http://www2.ed.gov/news/pressreleases/2009/08/08262009.html.

—. "K–8 Charter Schools: Closing the Achievement Gap." *Innovations in Education,* November 17, 2009. http://www2.ed.gov/admins/comm/choice/charterk-8/report_pg10.html.

—. "Overview Information; Race to the Top Fund; Notice Inviting Applications for New Awards for Fiscal Year (FY) 2010." *Federal Register,* vol. 74, no. 221 (November 18, 2009).

—. School Improvement Grants Application, Section 1003(g) of the Elementary and Secondary Education Act CFDA Numbers; 84.377A; 84.388A. OMB Number 1810-0682. June 30, 2010. http://www2.ed.gov/programs/sif/applicant.html.

Vernez, Georges, Scott Naftel, Karen Ross, Kerstin Carlson Le Floch, Christopher Beighley, and Brian Gill. *State and Local Implementation of the No Child Left Behind Act, Volume VII—Title I School Choice and Supplemental Educational Services: Final Report.* Jessup, MD: U.S. Department of Education, 2009, 13.

APPENDIX

Turnaround by the Numbers

Table A.1   Taft's turnaround: school proficiency and graduation rates, 2001–2010

School year	Grade 10 math (%)	Grade 10 reading (%)	Grade 10 writing (%)	Grade 10 science (%)	Grade 10 social studies (%)	Graduation rate (%)[a]
2001–2002[b]	33.3	68.2	70.9	40.8	53.9	25.3
2002–2003[b]	38.9	79.1	80.6	47.6	64.4	32.5
2003–2004[c]	29.0	58.9	93.0	49.5	61.9	55.2
2004–2005	40.0	64.3	47.0	14.8	26.1	76.2
2005–2006	86.7	91.3	67.3	36.0	88.0	62.3
2006–2007	90.3	91.6	74.8	70.3	85.9	88.5
2007–2008	95.9	98.8	69.9	90.3	97.2	89.3
2008–2009	97.9	97.9	79.8	93.5	96.8	95.2
2009–2010	96.2	96.2	83.1	93.5	94.7	95.2

[a]"Graduation rate" refers to black, non-Hispanic students who comprise more than 95 percent of the student body.
[b]Tests not directly comparable to current graduation tests
[c]Tests not directly comparable to current graduation tests

Sources: Ohio Department of Education; Elizabeth Holtzapple, and Jerry Moore, Cincinnati Public Schools.

Table A.2 Schools at a glance

School	District	Grades Enrolled	Number of students	Economically disadvantaged (%)	Black (%)	Hispanic (%)	Asian (%)	White (%)	Other (%)[a]	ELL (%)
Dr. Joseph Bellizzi Middle School[*b]	Hartford	5–8[c]	428	>95	16.4	78.3	2.1	3.3	0	26.2
Dr. Ramon E. Betances School[*d]	Hartford	preK–6[e]	439	>95	17.5	79.5	0.9	2.1	0	28.7
Bulkeley High School[*f]	Hartford	9–12	1,381	>95	22.2	69.5	1.4	6.6	0.3	22.7
Culinary Arts Academy[*g]	Hartford	10–12	221	>95	82.4	17.6	0	0	0	4.1
Dwight School[*h]	Hartford	preK–4	355	>95	19.7	70.4	1.7	8.2	0	20.1
Hartford Public High School[*i]	Hartford	9–12[j]	1,539	>95	35	60.3	2.5	1.9	0.3	23.6
High School Inc.[*k]	Hartford	9, 10+	200	n/a	n/a	n/a	n/a	n/a	n/a	n/a
Achievement First Hartford Academy Elementary School[†l]	Charter in Hartford	K–2+	266	63	98[m]	98[m]	n/a	n/a	n/a	n/a
Achievement First Hartford Academy Middle School[†n]	Charter in Hartford	5, 6+	175	65	99[o]	99[o]	n/a	n/a	n/a	n/a
Taft Information Technology High School[*p]	Cincinnati	9–12	506	68.4	95.6	0	0	2.9	0	25.5
Withrow University High School[*q]	Cincinnati	9–12	750	59.4	95.9	0	0	1.8	2.2	17.6
Brooklyn Generation School[*r]	New York	9, 10+	145	81	88	8	3	1	0	10.4
Garfield Middle School[†s]	Revere (MA)	6–8	423	82.7	4.7	54.1	9.9	26.5	4.7	53.7

Note: (+) symbol indicates school adding grades.
(*) symbol indicates data collected 2008–2009.
(†) symbol indicates data collected 2009–2010.

[a] In Hartford, "other" represents Native American.
[b] Opened Fall 2010 as Dwight-Bellizzi Asian Studies Academy.
[c] Grades reflect year of data.
[d] Closed; reopened Fall 2010 and Betances Early Literacy Lab School (preK–3).
[e] Grades reflect year of data.
[f] 2009–2010 divided into Bulkeley Lower and Bulkeley Upper Schools.
[g] Reopened in 2008; in 2009–2010 experienced some reorganization.
[h] Opened fall 2010 as Dwight-Bellizzi Asian Studies Academy.
[i] Opened fall 2008 as four academies including Law and Government; separate data not available at time of this printing.

[j] Data not separated by academy.
[k] Opened fall 2009; growing to 9–12; separate data not available at time of this printing.
[l] Opened fall 2008; growing to K–4.
[m] Data as reported by AF; not yet available from the state.
[n] Opened fall 2008; growing to 5–8.
[o] Data as reported by AF; not yet available from the state.
[p] Turnaround began in 2001; moving to new building December 2010.
[q] Turnaround began in 2002 as part of high-school-restructuring plan.
[r] Opened in 2008 with grade 9, growing to 9–12.
[s] Partnered with non-profit Citizen Schools beginning 2009–2010.

Table A.3 Grade 3—Betances and Dwight, 2009–2010

School	Math 2006	Math 2007	Math 2008	Math 2009	Math 2010	Reading 2006	Reading 2007	Reading 2008	Reading 2009	Reading 2010	Writing 2006	Writing 2007	Writing 2008	Writing 2009	Writing 2010
Betances	20.4	59.6	46.4	61.4	82	14.8	26.8	16.4	34.5	31	29.8	63.2	51.8	53.4	44
Dwight	56.8	57.0	59.4	77.4	74	37.0	43.8	42.2	77.4	60	75.3	78.8	77.4	90.6	80
State average	78.3	80.1	80.7	82.8	83.6	69.2	69.3	68.4	71.1	72.3	81.7	82.4	82.9	83.2	80.3

Table A.4 Hartford progress report compared to state

Year	Grade 3 Math	Grade 3 Reading	Grade 6 Math	Grade 6 Reading	Grade 8 Math	Grade 8 Reading	Grade 10 Math	Grade 10 Reading
Hartford								
2007	48.3	30.3	55.3	44.4	47.8	45.4	43.4	49.8
2008	49.9	33.5	60.1	47.9	47.0	45.2	46.7	52.2
2009	56.3	37.7	64.1	50.8	53.8	51.4	45.4	52.6
2010	61.4	45.7	71.8	64.8	63.1	59.5	52.2	64.3
Percent improvement over three years	**27.1**	**50.8**	**29.8**	**45.9**	**32.0**	**31.0**	**20.2**	**29.1**
State average								
2007	80.1	69.3	82.7	75.7	80.8	76.4	77.3	79.7
2008	80.7	68.4	84.3	77.6	81.2	77.0	79.7	82.7
2009	82.8	71.1	86.8	80.3	84.5	80.5	78.4	81.8
2010	83.6	72.3	88.2	85.5	86.6	82.6	78.8	82.9
Percent improvement over three years	**4.3**	**4.3**	**6.6**	**12.9**	**7.1**	**8.1**	**1.9**	**4.0**

Average three-year improvement of selected grades/tests:

Hartford: 33.2%

State average: 5.6%

Note: Scores are percentages of students scoring proficient or higher.

Table A.5 High school performance, 2009–2010

School	District	Graduation rate (%)	Grade 10 reading	Grade 10 math	Grade 10 writing	Grade 10 social studies	Grade 10 science (%)	Mean SAT (reading and math)
Taft Information Technology High School	Cincinnati	95.2	96.2	96.2	83.1	94.7	93.5	674[a]
Withrow University High School	Cincinnati	97.5	73.2	69.3	75.7	66.7	56.6	846[b]
Hartford Public High School[c]	Hartford	66.3	36.5	29.1	48.0	n/a	22.6	758
Law and Government Academy[d]	Hartford	n/a	53	31	65	n/a	24	890.5
High School Inc.[e]	Hartford	n/a	44	20	50	n/a	35	n/a
Hartford Culinary Academy[f]	Hartford	n/a	51.5	37.5	46.9	n/a	50	n/a
Bulkeley High School[g]	Hartford	76.7	70.9	75.5	65.1	n/a	56	767
Brooklyn Generation[h]	New York	n/a	n/a	42[i]	n/a	76[i]	n/a	n/a

[a]SAT scores are for 2008–2009.

[b]SAT scores are for 2008–2009.

[c]Includes three academies. Test scores for 2008–2009.

[d]Data from school principal and district.

[e]First year the school was open.

[f]Test scores rose dramatically in 2009–2010; proficient in 2008–2009= 24.7% in reading; 15.2% math; 39.7% writing; 19.5% science.

[g]Bulkeley High School has been split into Lower and Upper Schools; this data reflects both schools (Lower for state test scores; Upper for graduation/SAT data, etc.).

[h]Percentage is of students scoring 65 or better as required to earn graduation credit; scores were down from 2008–2009 (69% math and 83% social studies) because state raised standards requiring more correct answers to score a passing grade.

[i]These Regents exams are not easily compared with traditional state graduation tests. Students take a series of Regents tests throughout their high school careers.

Table A.6   The gap

District/ community	Per capita income	Adults with a BA or higher (%)	Adults without a high school diploma (%)	Kindergartners who attended preschool or Headstart (%)
Hartford	$13,428	20	38.7	34.2
Darien	$77,519	72	5.1	99.2
Greenwich	$74,346	62	8.5	94.2
New Canaan	$82,049	73	4.5	100
Weston	$74,817	75	2.8	97.9
Westport	$73,664	71	4.3	90.8

District/ community	Minorities in school district (%)	Students not fluent in English (%)	District graduation rate (%)	Grade 3 reading proficient (%)
Hartford	93.8	17.4	77.1	45.7
Darien	5.7	0.9	100	89.2
Greenwich	25	6.8	97	87.3
New Canaan	5.7	0.5	98.9	96.9
Weston	7	0.8	100	86.1
Westport	8	1.5	99.2	90.1

District/ community	Grade 3 math proficient (%)	Grade 8 reading proficient (%)	Grade 8 math proficient (%)	Grade 10 reading (%)
Hartford	61.4	59.5	63.1	64.3
Darien	95.8	94.4	98.1	97.2
Greenwich	92.5	90	91.9	94.6
New Canaan	96.6	96.3	99.7	99.1
Weston	95.7	97	97	99.5
Westport	94.5	96.2	98.6	98.8

District/ community	Grade 10 math (%)	Grads to higher ed (%)	SAT Math	SAT reading	SAT writing
Hartford	52.2	87.9	389	391	394
Darien	95.9	93.1	598	577	503
Greenwich	91.2	89.7	564	558	563
New Canaan	98.2	95.4	599	581	583
Weston	97.8	96.3	595	594	601
Westport	97.2	97.3	582	583	592

Sources: Connecticut Economic Resource Center; Connecticut State Department of Education Strategic School Profiles, 2007–2008 (latest available); Connecticut Mastery Test (CMT), grades 3–8; Connecticut Academic Performance Test (CAPT), grade 10 2010 test data.

DISCUSSION QUESTIONS

IN CHAPTER 1, Law and Government Academy principal Adam Johnson struggles with a key question: How should he handle students who aren't trying and who are not "cutting it" in the school? Is it fair to the students who are taking advantage of turnaround to acquire better educations and opportunities? It is easy to feel that students like Danny Contreras, who borrowed a computer programming text to read over Christmas vacation (chapter 7), "deserves" a quality education. But what about students who are less inspired, or simply uninterested? Is there a point beyond which schools should not be expected to reach a student, or does this run counter to the very idea of turnaround and educational equity?

*   *   *

HARTFORD SUPERINTENDENT Steven Adamowski (chapter 2) believes that uniforms and partners help connect student academic learning to the real world. Do you think having students wear dress shoes and ties really makes a difference? Why is it important? What role can partners play in strengthening urban schools? What partners might be tapped in your community?

*   *   *

CHAPTER 3 DISCUSSES the closing of the Ramon E. Betances School in Hartford at the end of the 2009–2010 school year. Although the school had made some academic progress and was less chaotic than a few years earlier, test scores and improvements were behind district targets (described in chapter 2). District leaders opted to redesign the school, upsetting the acting principal and faculty who had embraced a data-driven approach and were committed to turning around performance themselves. Would you have closed Betances? Why or why not?

*   *   *

THIS BOOK INCLUDES some very strong leaders who have strikingly different leadership styles from one another. In chapter 4, Sharon Johnson in Cincinnati believes in the school as "family" approach, and embraces the mother role, while Terrell Hill in Hartford talks tough to kids and their parents, staying on them as a way of getting them to step up and find capabilities in themselves. Is there any style you believe is more or less effective? What leads you to that conclusion? Do different grade levels and school environments call for different leadership styles?

* * *

IN CHAPTER 4, Dwight principal Stacey McCann has the task of combining her high-performing elementary school with a low-performing middle school as part of a turnaround strategy to create the Dwight-Bellizzi Asian Studies Academy (opened in fall 2010). In October 2009, the regularly scheduled joint staff meeting falls on the day when the district has issued bonus checks to teachers and staff at high-performing schools. McCann decides to go ahead and pass out the checks to the Dwight staff, who have earned them, obviously bypassing the Bellizzi staff, who did not earn bonus pay. This created an obvious spectacle that McCann chose not to avoid. Would you do the same thing? Why or why not?

* * *

TOP-PERFORMING URBAN charter schools like Achievement First have a full-time staff of recruiters to find teacher candidates. In chapter 4, Achievement First founder Dacia Toll describes how their approach presumes much on-the-job learning and growth among new teacher hires. In contrast, while district schools do schedule regular professional development, they assume teachers arrive with more teaching experience and skills. What do you see as the pros and cons of each approach in a turnaround setting? How can teachers from these different training backgrounds best work together?

* * *

AS DESCRIBED IN CHAPTER 5, Anthony Smith, principal of Taft Information Technology High School, began his turnaround by walking door to door and asking for support from the community. He also made clear that his "covenant" was with the community, not the board of education. Why is community support so important for failing schools? What can the community offer students that a school board cannot? How might these two sources of support work together more effectively?

* * *

IN A SCENE at the end of chapter 5, teacher Bridget Allison at Hartford Public High School's Law and Government Academy describes being on the cusp of exhaustion at the very moment that a former student visits to share his success—and to thank her. How familiar is this experience to you? How common is the push-pull between feeling utterly used up—and determined to alter the opportunities for your students? What fuels your commitment when your energy is exhausted? How central is teacher passion and energy to school turnaround?

* * *

THE CORPORATE-SCHOOL relationship is not always easy to navigate because of wants and expectations on both sides. In chapter 6, Jack Cassidy of Cincinnati Bell makes the point that you need "to go big or stay home," and so gives students his cell phone number in case of emergency. He says the company has actually given relatively few actual dollars but supports the school through its volunteer efforts (tutoring programs, organizing fundraisers, painting classrooms) and access to laptops, cell phones, and internet access—the company's core business. Do you think Jack Cassidy's approach to supporting Taft students is more helpful than if he were to just make a large corporate dollar donation? Why or why not?

* * *

CITIZEN SCHOOLS CEO Eric Schwarz (chapter 6) says that good nonprofit partners can help schools network more effectively—even with their own parents. Administrators at Garfield Middle School in Revere sound grateful for the regular phone calls to parents made by Citizen Schools' staff. Does it make sense, in effect, to outsource something as basic as parent-school communication? Is this a pragmatic solution for time-starved school leaders? Have you tried any alternative approaches to better connect with parents given that teacher time seems scarcer?

AT THE END of chapter 7, Hartford Public High School Nursing Academy senior Shaquana Cochran admits to being a poor student who was about to drop out when a key connection with a teacher helped her reengage in school and turn around her life plans. The value of teacher-student connections is a frequent and powerful theme in urban success stories. How does the current turnaround environment support—or fail to support—such mentoring relationships?

* * *

WHICH SCHOOL FEATURED in this book would you most like to work in? Why?

* * *

WAS THERE ANY school leader, district administrator, or teacher described in this book whose challenges or style particularly resonated with you? What attracts you to these leaders, and why? Are there leaders you would have found it difficult to work with? Why?

* * *

LEADING TURNAROUND AT the school level requires a willingness to think and act on the fly and sometimes diverge from the prescribed plan. How much latitude should district leaders allow principals? How patient should district leaders be in expecting results? Is three years enough to show progress? Why or why not? Have you seen examples in your school or district of midstream changes that you thought were surprising, but effective?

* * *

SCHOOL TURNAROUND IS difficult and uncertain—but exciting—work. Not every school faces extreme gaps, and yet there may be lessons to take from the experiences of those on the front lines. Is there anything that struck you as something you could use in your own school or district? What challenges or opportunities do you see ahead in applying these "takeaways" to your own situation? Are there any dilemmas described in the book that sound familiar to you or that resonate with your own front-line experience?

ABOUT THE
AUTHOR

Laura Pappano is an award-winning journalist who has been writing about education for more than two decades. The author of *The Connection Gap* (Rutgers University Press, 2001), and coauthor with Eileen McDonagh of *Playing With the Boys: Why Separate is Not Equal in Sports* (Oxford University Press, 2008), she is writer-in-residence at the Wellesley Centers for Women.

INDEX